MY INSTANT POT RECIPES 2022

EVERYDAY DELICIOUS SLOW COOKING RECIPES FOR BEGINNERS

DANIEL ROTH

Table of Contents

Brown Beef Stock Recipe 10

Beef Pepper Stock Recipe 12

Salmon Fish Stock Recipe 14

Roasted Tomato Sauce Recipe 16

Chicken with Herbs Stock Recipe 18

Cashew Cheese Sauce Recipe 20

Tunisian Chickpea Stock Recipe 22

Marinara Sauce Recipe 24

Chicken Kale Stock Recipe 26

Sweet Caramel Dipping Sauce Recipe 27

Super Quick Garlic Sauce Recipe 28

Sauce Recipe 29

Chicken Mushroom Stock Recipe 31

Seafood Gumbo Stock Recipe 33

Tomato and Crab Stock Recipe 35

Fish Anchovy Stock Recipe 37

Tomato Basil Sauce Recipe 38

Barbeque Sauce Recipe 40

Mushroom and Corn Stock Recipe 42

Orange Cranberry Sauce 44

Apple Cranberry Sauce	45
Rosemary Cranberry Apple Sauce	46
Apple Strawberry Sauce	47
Pumpkin Apple Cinnamon Sauce	48
Chicken Bone Broth	49
Leftover Turkey Stock	50
Bolognese Sauce	51
Spicy Beef Stock	52
Chicken Thyme Stock	54
Spicy Lamb Stock	55
Classic Beef Stock	57
Celery Lamb Stock	58
Butter Cheese Sauce	59
Cheese Onion Sauce	61
Enchilada Sauce	62
Curry Tomato Sauce	64
Mesan Basil Sauce	66
Tomato Goat Cheese Sauce	68
Marinara Sauce	70
Onion Apple Sauce	72
Pasta Sauce	74
Green Hot Sauce	76
Mushroom Sauce	78
Garlic Sauce	80

Special BBQ Sauce	82
Watermelon BBQ Sauce	84
Bolognese Bacon Sauce	86
Cashews Sauce	88
Strawberry Sauce	90
Cranberry Sauce	92
Roasted Tomato Sauce	94
Tomato Basil Sauce	96
Bolognese Eggplant Sauce	98
Beets Tomato Sauce	100
Bolognese Lentil Sauce	102
Apple Cinnamon Sauce	104
Spicy Indian Sauce	106
Instant Marinara Sauce	108
Potato and Shrimp Salad	110
Cheesy Artichokes Spread	112
Endives Platter	113
Crunchy Mushrooms	114
Wrapped Shrimp	116
Lentils Spread	118
Paprika Cranberry Dip	119
Citrus Onion Spread	120
Zucchini and Squash Dip	121
Garlic Cauliflower Dip	123

Broccoli Spread	125
Cumin Cheese Spread	126
Leeks and Bell Pepper Spread	128
Chicken, Spinach and Avocado Salad	130
Pesto Barley Bowls	131
Balsamic Olives Salsa	132
Cheese Dip with Peppers	133
Juicy Chicken Drumettes	134
Creamy Cauliflower Bites	135
Yummy Baby Carrots	137
Cheesy Keto Dip	138
Simple Brussels Sprouts	140
Quick Spinach Dip	141
Asparagus with Mayo Dip	142
Keto Greens Dip	143
Cocktail Sausages Asian-Style	145
Stuffed Mushrooms with Cheese	147
Family Meatballs	149
Fresh Keto Meatballs	151
Preparation Time: 20 minutes	153
Delicious Cauliflower Tots	155
Keto Broccoli Balls	157
Cheesy Taco Dip	158
Meatballs with Cheese	160

Spanish Fat Bombs 162
Yummy Cocktail Wieners 164
Fresh Brussels Sprouts with Aioli Sauce 166
Cheesy Bacon Bites 167
Juicy Meatballs 169
Perfect Chicken Wings 171
2-Ingredients Chicken Wings 173
Sticky Chicken Wings 175
Simple Boiled Peanuts 177
Southern Boiled Peanuts 179
Hard Boiled Eggs 181
Steamed Artichokes 182
Zingy Boiled Peanuts 184
Unique Party Food 186
Decadent Liver Pâté 188
Exotic Mushroom Pâté 190
Garden Fresh Salsa 192
Party Meatballs 194
Cheese Loaded Burgers 196
Mini Sausage Bites 198
Refreshing Curd 200
The Best Jam Ever 201
Divine Pears 202
Berry Marmalade 203

Orange Delight 204

Simple Squash Pie 205

Winter Pudding 207

Banana Dessert 209

Apple Cake 211

Special Vanilla Dessert 213

Tasty and Amazing Pear Dessert 214

Cranberries Jam 215

Lemon Jam 216

Special Dessert 217

Brown Beef Stock Recipe

Preparation Time: 2 hours 11 minutes

Servings: 10

Ingredients:

- 4 lb. beef stock bones
- 2 tbsp. olive oil
- 1 tbsp. apple cider vinegar
- 1 sprig fresh parsley
- 1 celery stalk; chopped into thirds
- 1 small onion; unpeeled and halved
- 2 garlic cloves; chopped.
- 1 tsp. dried bay leaf
- 1/2 tsp. whole black peppercorns
- 1 tsp. kosher salt

Directions:

1. Grease a baking tray with olive oil and place the beef bones on it.
2. Roast the bones for 30 minutes in an oven at 420 F. Flip the bones over and roast for another 20 minutes
3. Fill the instant pot with water up to one inch below the max line

4. Add all the ingredients: including the roasted beef bones, to the water.
5. Secure the lid. Turn the pressure release handle to the *sealed* position.
6. Select the *Manual* function; set to high pressure and adjust the time to 75 minutes
7. When it beeps; *Natural Release* the steam for 10 minutes and open the instant pot lid.
8. Strain the prepared stock through a mesh strainer and discard all the solids, Skim off all the surface fats and serve hot.

Beef Pepper Stock Recipe

Preparation Time : 2 hours 11 minutes

Servings: 10

Ingredients:

- 4 lb. beef stock bones
- 1 cup red bell pepper
- 2 tbsp. olive oil
- 2 garlic cloves; chopped.
- 1/4 tsp. red pepper flakes
- 1 celery stalk; chopped into thirds
- 1 small onion; unpeeled and halved
- 1/2 tsp. whole black peppercorns
- 1/4 tsp. turmeric ground
- 1 tsp. kosher salt

Directions:

1. Grease the baking tray with olive oil and place the beef bones on it
2. Roast the bones for 30 minutes in an oven at 420 F. Flip the bones over and roast for another 20 minutes
3. Fill the instant pot with water up to one inch below the max line.

4. Add all the ingredients: including the roasted beef bones to the water.
5. Secure the lid. Turn the pressure release handle to the *sealed* position.
6. Select the *Manual* function; set to high pressure and adjust the time to 75 minutes
7. When it beeps; *Natural Release* the steam for 10 minutes and open the instant pot lid.
8. Strain the prepared stock through a mesh strainer and discard all the solids, Skim off all the surface fats and serve hot.

Salmon Fish Stock Recipe

Preparation Time: 59 minutes

Servings: 6

Ingredients:

- 2 salmon heads 2 to 2½ lb.
- 6 cups cold water
- 1 cup dry white wine
- 1 carrot; diced
- 1 bay leaf
- 3 sprigs fresh thyme
- 1 small onion; quartered
- 2 cloves garlic
- 5 peppercorns

Directions:

1. Put the oil and the salmon heads in the instant pot and *Sauté* for 5 minutes
2. Pour the water into the pot.
3. Add all the remaining Ingredients to the water
4. Close the instant pot lid and turn the pressure release handle to the sealed position.
5. Select the *Manual* function; set to high pressure and adjust the timer to 48 minutes

6. When it beeps; *Natural Release* the steam for 10 minutes and open the instant pot lid.
7. Strain the prepared stock through a mesh strainer and discard all the solids, Skim off all the surface fats and serve hot.

Roasted Tomato Sauce Recipe

Preparation Time: 20 minutes

Servings: 4

Ingredients:

- 28 oz. canned; fire-roasted, diced tomatoes
- 1 red onion; chopped.
- 4 chipotle chilies in adobo sauce
- 2 tsp. powdered cumin
- 4 tsp. Mexican red chili powder
- 4 tsp. salt
- 1 green bell pepper, chopped.
- 1 jalapeño pepper; sliced
- 8 garlic cloves

- 1 cup water

Directions:

1. Put all the Ingredients in the instant pot.
2. Close the instant pot lid and turn the pressure release handle to the *sealed* position.
3. Select the *Manual* function; set to high pressure and adjust the timer to 10 minutes
4. When it beeps; *Quick Release* the steam and open the instant pot lid.
5. Transfer the sauce to a blender and blend well to form a smooth mixture Use immediately or save in a bottle for later use.

Chicken with Herbs Stock Recipe

Preparation Time: 66 minutes

Servings: 8

Ingredients:

- 2½ lb. chicken (bones only)
- 1 small onion; unpeeled and halved
- 1 tsp. dried bay leaf
- 1 sprig fresh parsley
- 1/2 tsp. whole black peppercorns
- 1/4 tsp. oregano
- 1/4 tsp. dried basil
- 8 cups water

- 1 tsp. sea salt

Directions:

1. Pour the water into the instant pot.
2. Put all the Ingredients into the water
3. Close the instant pot lid and turn the pressure release handle to the *sealed* position.
4. Select the *Manual* function; set on high pressure and adjust the timer to 60 minutes
5. When it beeps; *Natural Release* the steam for 10 minutes and open the instant pot lid.
6. Strain the prepared stock through a mesh strainer and discard all the solids, Skim off all the surface fats and serve hot.

Cashew Cheese Sauce Recipe

Preparation Time: 15 minutes

Servings: 5

Ingredients:

- 3/4 cup Yukon Gold potatoes; peeled and chopped.
- 1/4 white onion; peeled and quartered
- 1 garlic clove; peeled
- 1/2 cup carrots; peeled and sliced
- 1 tbsp. mellow white miso
- 1/2 tsp. smoked or sweet paprika
- 1 tbsp. lemon juice
- 1/4 cup raw cashews
- 1/4 cup nutritional yeast
- 1 cup water
- 1 tbsp. apple cider vinegar
- 1 tsp. sea salt

Directions:

1. Put all the Ingredients into the instant pot
2. Close the instant pot lid and turn the pressure release handle to the *sealed* position.
3. Select the *Manual* function; set to high pressure and adjust the timer to 5 minutes
4. When it beeps; *Quick Release* the steam and open the instant pot lid.
5. Transfer the sauce to a blender and blend well to form a smooth mixture. Use immediately or save in a bottle for later use.

Tunisian Chickpea Stock Recipe

Preparation Time: 30 minutes

Servings: 8

Ingredients:

- 1 cup carrots; diced
- 2 cups chickpeas; rinsed and drained
- 1/2 tsp. apple cider vinegar
- 1 tbsp. thyme leaves
- 1/2 tsp. red pepper flakes
- 1/2 cup green onions; chopped.
- 1 tsp. dried bay leaf
- 8 cups water

- 1 tsp. kosher salt

Directions:

1. Pour the water into the instant pot.
2. Put all the Ingredients into the water. Close the instant pot lid and turn the pressure release handle to the *sealed* position.
3. Select the *Manual* function. Set to high pressure and adjust the timer to 20 minutes
4. When it beeps; *Natural Release* the steam for 10 minutes and open the instant pot lid.
5. Strain the prepared stock through a mesh strainer and discard all the solids, Serve hot.

Marinara Sauce Recipe

Preparation Time: 26 minutes

Servings: 6

Ingredients:

- 2 cloves garlic; minced
- 2 small onions; chopped.
- 2 carrots; diced
- 4 cans tomatoes; diced
- 2 tbsp. butter; unsalted
- 4 tbsp. olive oil
- 3 tsp. dried basil
- 3 tsp. dried oregano
- Parsley; fresh
- 1½ tsp. sea salt
- freshly ground black pepper to taste

Directions:

1. Pour the oil into the instant pot and select the *Sauté* function.
2. Put all the vegetables into the oil and stir-fry for 5 minutes
3. Now put all the remaining ingredients: except the butter and black pepper, into the instant pot.
4. Close the instant pot lid and turn the pressure release handle to the *sealed* position.
5. Select the *Manual* function, set to high pressure and adjust the timer to 10 minutes
6. When it beeps; *Quick Release* the steam and open the instant pot lid.
7. Use an immerse blender to blend the sauce into a smooth paste
8. Add the butter and black pepper and cook for 1 minute on the *Sauté* function. Stir well and serve with pasta.

Chicken Kale Stock Recipe

Preparation Time: 66 minutes

Servings: 8

Ingredients:

- 2½ lb. chicken (bones only
- 1 small onion; unpeeled and halved
- 1 tsp. dried bay leaf
- 1 celery stalk; chopped into thirds
- 1 sprig fresh kale
- 8 cups water
- Salt and black pepper to taste

Directions:

1. Pour the water into the instant pot.
2. Put all the Ingredients into the water. Close the instant pot lid and turn the pressure release handle to the *sealed* position.
3. Select the *Manual* function; set on high pressure and adjust the timer to 60 minutes
4. When it beeps; *Natural Release* the steam for 10 minutes and open the instant pot lid.
5. Strain the prepared stock through a mesh strainer and discard all the solids, Skim off all the surface fats and serve hot.

Sweet Caramel Dipping Sauce Recipe

Preparation Time: 60 minutes

Servings: 4

Ingredients:

- 2 (14 oz. cans sweetened condensed milk
- 6 (3 oz. canning jars
- 1 cup water

Directions:

1. Pour the cup of water into the instant pot and place the trivet inside
2. Pour the condensed milk into the canning jars, Place the jars on the trivet.
3. Close the instant pot lid and turn the pressure release handle to the *sealed* position.
4. Select the *Manual* function; set to high pressure and adjust the timer to 50 minutes
5. When it beeps; *Quick Release* the steam and open the instant pot lid. Stir each jar and store in the refrigerator for later use.

Super Quick Garlic Sauce Recipe

Preparation Time: 8 minutes

Servings: 2

Ingredients:

- 1 cup water; (divided as explained in Preparation below
- 4 tbsp. chopped garlic
- 2 tbsp. chopped fresh parsley
- 4 tbsp. cornstarch
- 2 tsp. garlic powder
- 4 cups heavy cream
- Salt and pepper to taste

Directions:

1. Put half the water, garlic, garlic powder, cream, salt and pepper in the instant pot
2. Close the instant pot lid and turn the pressure release handle to the *sealed* position.
3. Select the *Manual* function; set to high pressure and adjust the timer to 3 minutes
4. When it beeps; *Quick Release* the steam and open the instant pot lid.
5. Mix the cornstarch with the remaining water. Add this slurry to the garlic sauce, Stir in the parsley and serve.

Sauce Recipe

Preparation Time: 15 minutes

Servings: 6

Ingredients:

- 1/4 tbsp. black pepper; freshly ground
- 1/4 tbsp. onion powder
- 2½ tbsp. white sugar
- 1/2 oz. lemon juice
- 1/2 oz. Worcestershire sauce
- 2 oz. apple cider vinegar
- 1/4 tbsp. dry mustard powder
- 8 oz. Heinz ketchup
- 2½ tbsp. brown sugar
- 1/2 oz. light corn syrup
- 1/2 tbsp. jerk rub
- 4 oz. water

Directions:

1. Put all the Ingredients in the instant pot
2. Close the instant pot lid and turn the pressure release handle to the *sealed* position.
3. Select the *Manual* function; set to high pressure and adjust the time to 5 minutes
4. When it beeps; *Natural Release* the steam for 10 minutes and open the instant pot lid. Use immediately or save in a bottle for later use.

Chicken Mushroom Stock Recipe

Preparation Time: 66 minutes

Servings: 8

Ingredients:

- 1 cup cremini mushrooms; diced
- 2½ lb. chicken (bones only
- 1 tsp. dried bay leaf
- 1/2 tsp. white pepper
- 8 cups water
- 1/2 tsp. whole black peppercorns
- 1 leek; finely chopped.
- 1 small onion; unpeeled and halved
- 1 tsp. kosher salt

Directions:

1. Pour the water into the instant pot.
2. Put all the Ingredients into the water.
3. Close the instant pot lid and turn the pressure release handle to the *sealed* position.
4. Select the *Manual* function, set on high pressure and adjust the timer to 60 minutes
5. When it beeps; *Natural Release* the steam for 10 minutes and open the instant pot lid
6. Strain the prepared stock through a mesh strainer and discard all the solids, Skim off all the surface fats and serve hot.

Seafood Gumbo Stock Recipe

Preparation Time: 66 minutes

Servings: 8

Ingredients:

- 1/2 lb. crab shells
- 1/2 lb. shrimp shells
- 6 cups cold water
- 1 cup dry white wine
- 1 small onion; quartered
- 1 salmon head
- 1 bay leaf
- 3 sprigs fresh thyme
- 5 peppercorns
- 2 cloves garlic
- 1 carrot; diced

Directions:

1. Put the oil salmon head, crab shells and shrimp shells in the instant pot and *Sauté* for 5 minutes
2. Pour the water into the instant pot.
3. Add all the remaining Ingredients to the water.
4. Close the instant pot lid and turn the pressure release handle to the *sealed* position.
5. Select the *Manual* function, set to high pressure and adjust the timer to 48 minutes
6. When it beeps; *Natural Release* the steam for 10 minutes and open the instant pot lid.
7. Strain the prepared stock through a mesh strainer and discard all the solids, Skim off all the surface fats and serve hot.

Tomato and Crab Stock Recipe

Preparation Time: 1 hour 30 minutes

Servings: 8

Ingredients:

- 2 lb. crab shells
- 2 tbsp. tomato paste
- 1 onion; rough chop – skin on
- 4 cloves of garlic
- 1 tsp. black peppercorns
- 1 tsp. parsley flakes
- 2 bay leaves
- 1 cup carrots; rough chop
- 2 stalks of celery; rough chop
- 4 sprigs fresh thyme
- 10 cups water

Directions:

1. Put the oil crab shells and vegetables in the instant pot and *Sauté* for 5 minutes
2. Pour the water into the instant pot.
3. Add all the remaining Ingredients to the water.
4. Close the instant pot lid and turn the pressure release handle to the *sealed* position.
5. Select the *Manual* function, set to high pressure and adjust the timer to 80 minutes
6. When it beeps; *Natural Release* the steam for 10 minutes and open the instant pot lid.
7. Strain the prepared stock through a mesh strainer and discard all the solids, Serve

Fish Anchovy Stock Recipe

Preparation Time: 25 minutes

Servings: 8

Ingredients:

- 2 oz. dried anchovies
- 1/2 tsp. whole black peppercorns
- 8 cups water
- 1 celery stalk; chopped into thirds
- 6 small pieces kombu
- 1 tsp. kosher salt

Directions:

1. Pour the water into the instant pot.
2. Put all the Ingredients into the water.
3. Close the instant pot lid and turn the pressure release handle to the *sealed* position.
4. Select the *Manual* function. Set to high pressure and adjust the timer to 20 minutes
5. When it beeps; *Natural Release* the steam for 10 minutes and open the instant pot lid.
6. Strain the prepared stock through a mesh strainer and discard all the solids, Skim off all the surface fats and serve hot.

Tomato Basil Sauce Recipe

Preparation Time: 20 minutes

Servings: 8

Ingredients:

- 8 lb. Romas tomatoes; diced
- 1 cup chopped fresh basil
- 2 tbsp. salt
- 1 tbsp. pepper
- 1 tbsp. garlic powder
- 3 tbsp. Italian seasoning
- 4 tbsp. olive oil
- 1/2 garlic cloves; minced
- 2 onions; diced
- 1/2 tsp. crushed peppers
- 2 bay leaves

Directions:

1. Pour the oil into the instant pot and select the *Sauté* function.
2. Add the garlic and onions to the oil and stir-fry for 5 minutes
3. Now add all the remaining ingredients; except the basil to the instant pot.

4. Close the instant pot lid and turn the pressure release handle to the *sealed* position.
5. Select the *Manual* function; set to high pressure and adjust the timer to 10 minutes
6. When it beeps; *Quick Release* the steam and open the instant pot lid.
7. Stir well; remove the bay leaves and add the basil to the sauce, Serve

Barbeque Sauce Recipe

Preparation Time: 23 minutes

Servings: 5

Ingredients:

- 2 tbsp. sesame seed oil
- 2 tsp. hot sauce
- 2 medium onions; roughly chopped.
- 1/2 cup white vinegar
- 1 tsp. granulated garlic
- 2 tsp. liquid smoke
- 1/4 tsp. clove ground
- 1/4 tsp. cumin powder
- 1 cup tomato puree
- 1 cup water
- 1/2 cup honey
- 1½ cups seedless dried plums
- 2 tsp. sea salt

Directions:

1. Put the oil, onion and garlic into the instant pot and *Sauté* for 3 minutes,
2. Stir in all the Ingredients and mix them well
3. Close the instant pot lid and turn the pressure release handle to the *sealed* position.

4. Select the *Manual* function, set to high pressure and adjust the timer to 10 minutes
5. When it beeps; *Quick Release* the steam and open the instant pot lid.
6. Transfer the sauce to a blender and blend well to form a smooth mixture Use immediately or save in a bottle for later use.

Mushroom and Corn Stock Recipe

Preparation Time: 20 minutes

Servings: 8

Ingredients:

- 4 large mushrooms; diced
- 2 cobs of corns
- 1 celery stalk; chopped into thirds
- 1 tsp. ginger; grated
- 8 cups water
- 1 sprig fresh parsley
- 1/2 tsp. whole black peppercorns
- 1 small onion; unpeeled and halved
- 1 tsp. dried bay leaf
- 1/2 tsp. turmeric ground
- 1 tsp. kosher salt

Directions:

1. Pour the water into the instant pot.
2. Add all the Ingredients to the water
3. Close the instant pot lid and turn the pressure release handle to the *sealed* position.
4. Select the *Manual* function and set to high pressure, Adjust the time to 15 minutes
5. When it beeps; *Natural Release* the steam for 10 minutes and open the instant pot lid.
6. Strain the prepared stock through a mesh strainer and discard all the solids, Serve hot.

Orange Cranberry Sauce

Servings: 30

Cooking Time: 5 minutes

Ingredients:

- 12 oz cranberries
- ½ tsp orange zest
- 1 cup sugar
- 1 cup orange juice

Directions:

1. Add all ingredients into the instant pot and stir well.
2. Seal pot with lid and cook on high for 5 minutes.
3. Release pressure using quick release method than open the lid.
4. Allow to cool completely then store.
5. Nutritional Values per serving:
6. Calories: 35; Carbohydrates: 8.6g; Protein: 0.1g; Fat: 0g; Sugar: 7.8g; Sodium: 0mg

Apple Cranberry Sauce

Servings: 8

Cooking Time: 10 minutes

Ingredients:

- 1 apple, peeled, cored, and chopped
- ½ cup maple syrup
- ½ cup apple cider
- 1 orange zest
- 1 orange juice
- 12 oz fresh cranberries, rinsed

Directions:

1. Add all ingredients into the instant pot and stir well.
2. Seal pot with lid and cook on high for 5 minutes.
3. Allow to release pressure naturally for 5 minutes then release using quick release method.
4. Allow to cool completely and store.

Nutritional Values per serving:

Calories: 101; Carbohydrates: 23.9g; Protein: 0.2g; Fat: 0.1g; Sugar: 18.8g; Sodium: 3mg

Rosemary Cranberry Apple Sauce

Servings: 16

Cooking Time: 5 minutes

Ingredients:

- 2 lbs apples, cored and diced
- 2 tbsp maple syrup
- 1 fresh rosemary sprig
- 1 cup apple cider
- 12 oz cranberries

Directions:

1. Add all ingredients into the instant pot and stir well.
2. Seal pot with lid and cook on high for 5 minutes.
3. Release pressure using quick release method than open the lid.
4. Discard rosemary from the sauce and using masher mash until getting the desired consistency.
5. Allow to cool completely then store.

Nutritional Values per serving:

Calories: 40; Carbohydrates: 9.3g; Protein: 0.1g; Fat: 0.1g; Sugar: 6.9g; Sodium: 1mg

Apple Strawberry Sauce

Servings: 15

Cooking Time: 19 minutes

Ingredients:

- 6 apples, peeled, cored, and diced
- ¼ cup sugar
- 1 pear, peeled, cored, and diced
- 2 tbsp fresh lemon juice
- ¼ tsp cinnamon
- 2 cups strawberries

Directions:

1. Add all ingredients into the instant pot and stir well.
2. Seal pot with lid and cook on high for 4 minutes.
3. Allow to release pressure naturally for 15 minutes then release using quick release method.
4. Mash the sauce using masher until getting desired consistency.
5. Allow to cool completely and store.

Nutritional Values per serving:

Calories: 71; Carbohydrates: 18.6g; Protein: 0.4g; Fat: 0.3g; Sugar: 14.5g; Sodium: 2mg

Pumpkin Apple Cinnamon Sauce

Servings: 8

Cooking Time: 10 minutes

Ingredients:

- 2 ½ lbs apples, peeled, cored, and diced
- 2/3 cup water
- 2 ½ tbsp brown sugar
- 1 ½ tsp cinnamon
- 2/3 cup pumpkin puree

Directions:

1. Add all ingredients into the instant pot and stir well.
2. Seal pot with lid and cook on high for 5 minutes.
3. Allow to release pressure naturally for 5 minutes then release using quick release method.
4. Allow to cool completely and transfer in a jar.
5. Store in the refrigerator.

Nutritional Values per serving:

Calories: 55; Carbohydrates: 14.4g; Protein: 0.4g; Fat: 0.2g; Sugar: 10.7g; Sodium: 3mg

Chicken Bone Broth

Servings: 4

Cooking Time: 70 minutes

Ingredients:

- 1 chicken bones
- 6 cups water
- ¼ cup apple cider vinegar
- 1 tbsp sea salt

Directions:

1. Add all ingredients into the instant pot.
2. Seal pot with lid and cook on manual mode for 60 minutes.
3. Allow to release pressure naturally for 10 minutes then release using quick release method.
4. Strain the broth and store.

Nutritional Values per serving:

Calories: 38; Carbohydrates: 0.9g; Protein: 4.9g; Fat: 1.4g; Sugar: 0.7g; Sodium: 763mg

Leftover Turkey Stock

Servings: 4

Cooking Time: 70 minutes

Ingredients:

- 1 lb leftover turkey carcass
- 6 cups water
- 2 garlic cloves
- 1 cup carrots, sliced
- 1 cup celery, sliced
- 1 cup onion, diced

Directions:

1. Add all ingredients into the instant pot.
2. Seal pot with lid and cook on manual mode for 60 minutes.
3. Allow to release pressure naturally for 10 minutes then release using quick release method.
4. Strain the stock and store.

Nutritional Values per serving:

Calories: 10; Carbohydrates: 0.9g; Protein: 2g; Fat: 0g; Sugar: 0.9g; Sodium: 990mg

Bolognese Sauce

Servings: 4

Cooking Time: 8 minutes

Ingredients:

- 1 lb ground beef
- 1 ½ tsp garlic, minced
- 3 tbsp fresh parsley, chopped
- 14 oz marinara sauce

Directions:

1. Add all ingredients into the instant pot and stir well.
2. Seal pot with lid and cook on high for 8 minutes.
3. Release pressure using quick release method than open the lid.
4. Stir well and serve.

Nutritional Values per serving:

Calories: 300; Carbohydrates: 14.2g; Protein: 36.3g; Fat: 9.8g; Sugar: 8.8g; Sodium: 483mg

Spicy Beef Stock

Servings: 6

Cooking Time: 45 minutes

Ingredients:

- 2 lbs beef bones
- ½ tsp red pepper flakes
- 2 tsp chili pepper
- 3 tbsp red wine vinegar
- ¼ cup onions, chopped
- ¼ cup celery, chopped
- ¼ cup celery stalk, chopped
- 3 garlic cloves
- 3 chili peppers
- 1 tsp salt

Directions:

1. Add all ingredients to the pot and pour enough water to cover.
2. Seal pot with lid and cook on high for 35 minutes.
3. Allow to release pressure naturally for 10 minutes then release using quick release method.
4. Strain stock and store.

Nutritional Values per serving:

Calories: 17; Carbohydrates: 1.7g; Protein: 2g; Fat: 0.4g; Sugar: 0.6g; Sodium: 396mg

Chicken Thyme Stock

Servings: 4

Cooking Time: 35 minutes

Ingredients:

- 2 lbs chicken neck
- 1 tsp peppercorn
- 1 tsp dried thyme
- ½ cup fresh parsley, chopped
- 2 chicken thighs
- 2 tsp sea salt

Directions:

1. Add all ingredients to the pot and pour enough water to cover.
2. Seal pot with lid and cook on high for 25 minutes.
3. Allow to release pressure naturally for 10 minutes then release using quick release method.
4. Strain stock and store.

Nutritional Values per serving:

Calories: 12; Carbohydrates: 1g; Protein: 0.8g; Fat: 0.6g; Sugar: 0.1g; Sodium: 941mg

Spicy Lamb Stock

Servings: 5

Cooking Time: 6 hours 10 minute

Ingredients:

- 2 lbs lamb bones
- ½ tsp white pepper
- 1 tsp red pepper flakes
- 2 tsp chili powder
- ¼ cup red wine vinegar
- ¼ cup celery, chopped
- 5 garlic cloves
- 1 onion, sliced
- 1 tsp salt

Directions:

1. Add all ingredients into the instant pot and pour enough water to cover.
2. Seal pot with lid and cook on slow cook mode for 6 hours.
3. Allow to release pressure naturally for 10 minutes then release using quick release method.
4. Strain stock and store.

Nutritional Values per serving:

Calories: 24; Carbohydrates: 4.2g; Protein: 2.5g; Fat: 0.7g; Sugar: 1.2g; Sodium: 620mg

Classic Beef Stock

Servings: 4

Cooking Time: 45 minutes

Ingredients:

- 2 lbs beef bones
- ½ tsp dried basil
- 1 tsp peppercorns
- 4 garlic cloves
- ½ cup celery stalks, chopped
- 2 tbsp red wine vinegar
- 1 tsp sea salt

Directions:

1. Add all ingredients into the instant pot and pour enough water to cover.
2. Seal pot with lid and cook on high for 35 minutes.
3. Allow to release pressure naturally for 10 minutes then release using quick release method.
4. Strain stock and store.

Nutritional Values per serving:

Calories: 18; Carbohydrates: 1.8g; Protein: 2.3g; Fat: 0.4g; Sugar: 0.2g; Sodium: 479mg

Celery Lamb Stock

Servings: 4

Cooking Time: 15 minutes

Ingredients:

- 2 lbs lamb bones
- 1 tsp dried thyme
- 2 tbsp apple cider vinegar
- ½ cup celery leaves
- 2 celery stalks, chopped
- 2 onions, sliced
- 1 tsp salt

Directions:

1. Add all ingredients into the instant pot and pour enough water to cover.
2. Seal pot with lid and cook on high for 15 minutes.
3. Release pressure using quick release method than open the lid.
4. Strain stock and store.

Nutritional Values per serving:

Calories: 42; Carbohydrates: 6g; Protein: 3.4g; Fat: 0.6g; Sugar: 2.6g; Sodium: 773mg

Butter Cheese Sauce

Servings: 8

Cooking Time: 8 minutes

Ingredients:

- 1/3 cup butter
- ¼ tsp dried basil
- 1 tsp red chili flakes
- 1 cup vegetable stock
- 2 garlic cloves, crushed
- ¼ cup fresh parsley, chopped
- 2 tbsp parmesan cheese, grated
- 1 cup cottage cheese
- 2 cups cream cheese
- ½ tsp salt

Directions:

1. Add butter, basil, red chili flakes, and salt to the instant pot and set pot on sauté mode.
2. Once butter is melted then add garlic and sauté for a minute.
3. Add parmesan cheese, cottage cheese, and cream cheese and cook for 2 minutes.
4. Add parsley and stock. Stir well. Seal pot with lid and cook on manual mode for 6 minutes.

5. Release pressure using quick release method than open the lid.
6. Once sauce is cool completely then store in a jar.

Nutritional Values per serving:

Calories: 308; Carbohydrates: 3.2g; Protein: 9.2g; Fat: 29.3g; Sugar: 0.5g; Sodium: 617mg

Cheese Onion Sauce

Servings: 5

Cooking Time: 35 minutes

Ingredients:

- 1 onion, chopped
- 2 tsp dried parsley
- 1 tsp onion powder
- 2 tbsp olive oil
- 1 cup vegetable stock
- 2 cups cream cheese

Directions:

1. Add oil into the instant pot and set the pot on sauté mode.
2. Add onion and sauté for 10 minutes.
3. Add remaining ingredients and stir well.
4. Seal pot with lid and cook manual mode for 15 minutes.
5. Allow to release pressure naturally for 10 minutes then release using quick release method.
6. Allow to cool completely then store.

Nutritional Values per serving:

Calories: 385; Carbohydrates: 5.3g; Protein: 7.3g; Fat: 3804g; Sugar: 1.7g; Sodium: 420mg

Enchilada Sauce

Servings: 8

Cooking Time: 20 minutes

Ingredients:

- 14 oz can roasted tomatoes, diced
- ½ cup water
- 1 tsp red chili powder
- 2 chipotle chilies in adobo sauce
- 3 garlic cloves
- ½ jalapeno pepper, sliced
- ½ bell pepper, chopped
- ½ onion, chopped
- 1 tsp salt

Directions:

1. Add all ingredients except tomatoes into the instant pot and stir well.
2. Add tomatoes on top. Seal pot with lid and cook on high for 10 minutes.
3. Allow to release pressure naturally for 10 minutes then release using quick release method.
4. Using blender blend the sauce and store.

Nutritional Values per serving:

Calories: 20; Carbohydrates: 4.2g; Protein: 0.7g; Fat: 0.1g; Sugar: 1.9g; Sodium: 408mg

Curry Tomato Sauce

Servings: 8

Cooking Time: 13 minutes

Ingredients:

- 28 oz can tomatoes, crushed
- ½ cup can coconut milk
- ½ tsp black pepper
- 1 tbsp fresh thyme leaves
- ¼ tsp ground cinnamon
- ¼ tsp red pepper flakes
- ½ tsp turmeric
- ½ tsp garam masala
- 1 tbsp ginger, minced
- 3 garlic cloves
- ½ onion, diced
- 1 tsp sea salt

Directions:

1. Add all ingredients into the instant pot and stir well.
2. Seal pot with lid and cook on high for 10 minutes.
3. Release pressure using quick release method than open the lid.
4. Using blender blend the sauce until smooth.
5. Transfer sauce in container and store.

Nutritional Values per serving:

Calories: 58; Carbohydrates: 7.4g; Protein: 1.5g; Fat: 3.1g; Sugar: 3.7g; Sodium: 448mg

Mesan Basil Sauce

Servings: 5

Cooking Time: 15 minutes

Ingredients:

- 1 tbsp parmesan cheese
- ¼ tsp dried thyme
- ¼ tsp black pepper
- 1 tbsp olive oil
- 1 garlic clove, crushed
- ½ cup fresh basil
- ½ cup feta cheese, crumbled
- 1 cup cream cheese
- ½ tsp salt

Directions:

1. Add all ingredients into the heat-safe bowl and stir well.
2. Pour ½ cup of water into the instant pot than place a trivet in the pot.
3. Place bowl on top of the trivet. Seal pot with lid and cook on manual mode for 10 minutes.
4. Release pressure using quick release method than open the lid.
5. Remove bowl from the pot and set aside to cool completely.
6. Place in refrigerator for an hour. Serve chilled.

Nutritional Values per serving:

Calories: 232; Carbohydrates: 2.2g; Protein: 6.1g; Fat: 22.5g; Sugar: 0.7g; Sodium: 555mg

Tomato Goat Cheese Sauce

Servings: 4

Cooking Time: 3 hours

Ingredients:

- 1 cup goat cheese, crumbled
- ¼ tsp chili powder
- 1 tsp dried rosemary
- ¼ cup apple cider vinegar
- 3 tbsp olive oil
- 3 garlic cloves, crushed
- 1 onion, chopped
- ½ cup mozzarella cheese, shredded
- 1 cup tomatoes, diced

Directions:
1. Add all ingredients into the instant pot and stir well to combine.
2. Seal pot with lid and cook on slow cook mode for 3 hours.
3. Release pressure using quick release method than open the lid.
4. Allow to cool completely then serve.

Nutritional Values per serving:

Calories: 207; Carbohydrates: 6.6g; Protein: 6.9g; Fat: 18.3g; Sugar: 2.4g; Sodium: 162mg

Marinara Sauce

Servings: 8

Cooking Time: 17 minutes

Ingredients:

- ¼ cup water
- ¼ tsp red pepper flakes
- ½ tsp oregano
- ½ tsp thyme
- 3 tbsp fresh basil
- 1 carrot, peeled and grated
- 1 ¼ lbs tomatoes, crushed
- 3 garlic cloves, chopped
- 1 onion, chopped
- 1 tbsp olive oil
- Pepper
- Salt

Directions:

1. Add oil into the instant pot and set the pot on sauté mode.
2. Add garlic and onion and sauté for 2 minutes.
3. Add remaining ingredients and stir well.
4. Seal pot with lid and cook on high for 30 minutes.
5. Release pressure using quick release method than open the lid.
6. Using blender blend the sauce.
7. Allow to cool completely then store in a container.

Nutritional Values per serving:

Calories: 39; Carbohydrates: 5.3g; Protein: 1g; Fat: 1.9g; Sugar: 2.8g; Sodium: 29mg

Onion Apple Sauce

Servings: 8

Cooking Time: 55 minutes

Ingredients:

- 1 onion, chopped
- 2 apples, chopped
- ¼ tsp liquid stevia
- ¼ cup fresh cilantro, chopped
- 1 cup vegetable broth
- 2 tbsp butter
- ¼ cup apple cider vinegar
- ½ tsp salt

Directions:
1. Add butter into the instant pot and set the pot on sauté mode.
2. Add onion and apple to the pot and sauté for 10 minutes.
3. Add stevia, apple cider vinegar, and salt. Stir well.
4. Add broth and cilantro. Seal pot with lid and cook on manual mode for 35 minutes.
5. Allow to release pressure naturally for 10 minutes then release using quick release method.
6. Using blender puree the sauce until smooth.

Nutritional Values per serving:

Calories: 66; Carbohydrates: 9g; Protein: 1g; Fat: 3.2g; Sugar: 6.5g; Sodium: 265mg

Pasta Sauce

Servings: 12

Cooking Time: 33 minutes

Ingredients:

- 8 cups tomatoes, diced
- 1 tsp sugar
- 1 tsp pepper
- 1 ½ tbsp Italian seasoning
- 4 garlic cloves, minced
- 1 onion, diced
- 3 cups water
- 2 tbsp olive oil
- 1 tsp salt

Directions:

- Add oil into the instant pot and set the pot on sauté mode.
- Add garlic and onion and sauté for 2-3 minutes.
- Add remaining ingredients and stir well. Seal pot with lid and cook on high for 30 minutes.
- Release pressure using quick release method than open the lid.
- Puree the sauce using a blender.
- Serve over pasta and enjoy.

Nutritional Values per serving:

Calories: 54; Carbohydrates: 6.5g; Protein: 1.3g; Fat: 3.1g; Sugar: 4g; Sodium: 203mg

Green Hot Sauce

Serving: 8

Preparation Time: 5 minutes

Cooking Time: 02 minutes

Ingredients

- 16 oz. green chilies
- 8 garlic cloves, peeled and smashed
- 1 green bell pepper, chopped
- 1 cup white vinegar
- ¼ cup apple cider vinegar
- ½ cup water
- 1 tablespoon sea salt

Directions

1. 1.Put all the ingredients into the instant pot.
2. Secure the lid and turn the pressure release handle to the 'sealed' position.
3. Select the 'Manual' function. Set to high pressure and adjust the timer to 2 minutes.
4. After the beep, 'Quick release' the steam and remove the lid.
5. Transfer the sauce to a blender and blend well to form a smooth mixture.
6. Use immediately or save in a bottle for later use.

Nutrition Values Per Serving:

Calories: 34

Carbohydrate: 6.2g

Protein: 0.3g

Fat: 0.1g

Sugar: 2.8g

Sodium: 932mg

Mushroom Sauce

Serving: 3

Preparation Time: 5 minutes
Cooking Time: 08 minutes

Ingredients

- 1 tablespoon butter
- 2½ cups portabella mushrooms, sliced
- 1 sprig fresh thyme
- 1 garlic clove, crushed
- ½ cup cream
- ½ cup milk
- 3 teaspoons corn starch
- 1 tablespoon lemon juice
- Salt and pepper to taste
- ½ cup water
- 1 tablespoon chopped parsley

Directions

1. Select the 'sauté' function on the instant pot and heat the butter.
2. Add the garlic, mushrooms and thyme to the heated butter. Stir-fry for 5 minutes.
3. Add the salt, pepper, cream and water to the mushrooms.

4. Secure the lid and turn the pressure release handle to the 'sealed' position.
5. Select the 'manual' function, set to high pressure and adjust the timer to 3 minutes.
6. After the beep, 'quick release' the steam and remove the lid.
7. Prepare a slurry by mixing the corn-starch with half a cup of milk. Add this slurry to the mushroom sauce.
8. Stir in the parsley and lemon juice, then serve.

Nutrition Values Per Serving:

Calories: 69

Carbohydrate: 5.3g

Protein: 1.8g

Fat: 4.9g

Sugar: 2g

Sodium: 27mg

Garlic Sauce

Serving: 2

Preparation Time: 5 minutes

Cooking Time: 03 minutes

Ingredients

- 1 cup water, (divided as explained in Directions below
- 4 tablespoons chopped garlic
- 2 teaspoon garlic powder
- 4 cups heavy cream
- 2 tablespoon chopped fresh parsley
- Salt and pepper to taste
- 4 tablespoons cornstarch

Directions

1. Put half the water, garlic, garlic powder, cream, salt and pepper in the instant pot.
2. Secure the lid and turn the pressure release handle to the 'sealed' position.
3. Select the 'manual' function, set to high pressure and adjust the timer to 3 minutes.
4. After the beep, 'quick release' the steam and remove the lid.
5. Mix the corn-starch with the remaining water. Add this slurry to the garlic sauce.

6. Stir in the parsley and serve.

Nutrition Values Per Serving:

Calories: 231

Carbohydrate: 7.3g

Protein: 1.7g

Fat: 22.2g

Sugar: 0.3g

Sodium: 25mg

Special BBQ Sauce

Serving: 5

Preparation Time: 10 minutes

Cooking Time: 05 minutes

Ingredients

- 8 oz Heinz ketchup
- 1 cup water
- 2½ tablespoons brown sugar
- 2½ tablespoons white sugar
- ¼ tablespoon black pepper, freshly ground
- ¼ tablespoon onion powder
- ¼ tablespoon dry mustard powder
- ½ oz lemon juice
- ½ oz Worcestershire sauce
- 2 oz apple cider vinegar
- ½ oz light corn syrup
- ½ tablespoon jerk rub

Directions

1. Put all the ingredients in the instant pot.
2. Secure the lid and turn the pressure release handle to the 'sealed' position.
3. Select the 'manual' function, set to high pressure and adjust the time to 5 minutes.
4. After the beep, 'natural release' the steam for 10 minutes and remove the lid.
5. Use immediately or save in a bottle for later use.

Nutrition Values Per Serving:

Calories: 85

Carbohydrate: 21.1g

Protein: 0.5g

Fat: 0.2g

Sugar: 18.6g

Sodium: 475mg

Watermelon BBQ Sauce

Serving: 8

Preparation Time: 15 minutes

Cooking Time: 20 minutes

Ingredients

- 2 cups watermelon pulp
- 2 cups dark corn syrup
- ½ cup watermelon juice
- ½ cup Heinz ketchup
- ½ cup distilled vinegar
- ½ teaspoon crushed red pepper flakes
- 1 teaspoon liquid smoke
- ½ teaspoon freshly ground black pepper

Directions

1. Put the diced, red part of the watermelon into a food processor and blend.
2. Strain the watermelon pulp from its water. Keep it aside for later use.
3. Put all the ingredients, including 1 cup watermelon pulp, in the instant pot.
4. Secure the lid and turn the pressure release handle to the 'sealed' position.

5. Select the 'manual' function, set to high pressure and adjust the timer to 20 minutes.
6. After the beep, 'natural release' the steam for 10 minutes and remove the lid.
7. Let it simmer for 5 minutes.
8. Use immediately or save in a jar for later use.

Nutrition Values Per Serving:

Calories: 244

Carbohydrate: 64.9g

Protein: 0.3g

Fat: 0.1g

Sugar: 25.6g

Sodium: 170mg

Bolognese Bacon Sauce

Serving: 6

Preparation Time: 5 minutes

Cooking Time: 45 minutes

Ingredients

- ½ large onion, finely chopped
- 1 carrot, finely chopped
- 1½ celery stalks, finely chopped
- 1½ garlic cloves, minced or pressed
- ½ tablespoon olive oil
- ½ (6 oz. can tomato paste
- 1 lb ground beef
- ½ cup bacon, diced
- ½ tablespoon salt
- ½ teaspoon black pepper
- ¾ teaspoon dried thyme
- 1 teaspoon dried oregano
- 1 (28 oz can crushed tomatoes
- 1 cup whole milk
- 1 cup dry red wine
- Pasta for serving

Directions

1. Pour the oil into the instant pot and select the 'sauté' function.
2. Add all the vegetables to the oil and stir-fry for 10 minutes.
3. Stir in the tomato paste and all the spices. Use an immerse blender to blend the sauce.
4. Now put all the remaining ingredients into the instant pot.
5. Secure the lid and turn the pressure release handle to the 'sealed' position.
6. Select the 'meat stew' function and adjust the timer to 35 minutes.
7. After the beep, 'quick release' the steam and remove the lid.
8. Stir well and serve with pasta.

Nutrition Values Per Serving:

Calories: 322

Carbohydrate: 25.8g

Protein: 29.7g

Fat: 7.9g

Sugar: 16.3g

Sodium: 978mg

Cashews Sauce

Serving: 4

Preparation Time: 10 minutes

Cooking Time: 05 minutes

Ingredients

- 1 cup water
- ¼ white onion, peeled and quartered
- 1 garlic clove, peeled
- ½ cup carrots, peeled and sliced
- ¾ cup Yukon Gold potatoes, peeled and chopped
- ¼ cup raw cashews
- ¼ cup nutritional yeast
- 1 tablespoon mellow white miso
- ½ teaspoon smoked or sweet paprika
- 1 tablespoon lemon juice
- 1 tablespoon apple cider vinegar
- 1 teaspoon sea salt

Directions

1. Add all the ingredients into the instant pot.
2. Secure the lid and turn the pressure release handle to the 'sealed' position.
3. Select the 'Manual' function, set to high pressure and adjust the timer to 5 minutes.

4. After the beep, 'Quick release' the steam and remove the lid.
5. Transfer the sauce to a blender and blend well to form a smooth mixture.
6. Use immediately or save in a bottle for later use.

Nutrition Values Per Serving:

Calories: 103

Carbohydrate: 13.4g

Protein: 5.5g

Fat: 3.7g

Sugar: 1.4g

Sodium: 501mg

Strawberry Sauce

Serving: 5

Preparation Time: 02 minutes

Cooking Time: 08 minutes

Ingredients

- 8 oz. fresh strawberries
- 2 tablespoons raw honey
- ½ cup pure squeezed orange juice
- ½ teaspoon cinnamon or 2 cinnamon sticks
- 1 tablespoon stevia

Directions

1. Put all the ingredients in the instant pot.
2. Secure the lid and turn the pressure release handle to the 'sealed' position.
3. Select the 'Manual' function, set to high pressure and adjust the timer to 8 minutes.
4. After the beep, 'Quick release' the steam and remove the lid.
5. Use an immerse blender to puree the sauce.
6. Serve when cool, or save in a bottle for later use.

Nutrition Values Per Serving:

Calories: 63

Carbohydrate: 15.6g

Protein: 0.5g

Fat: 0.1g

Sugar: 13.9g

Sodium: 4mg

Cranberry Sauce

Serving: 5

Preparation Time: 2 minutes

Cooking Time: 08 minutes

Ingredients

- 8 oz. fresh cranberries
- 2 tablespoons raw honey
- ½ cup pure squeezed orange juice
- ½ teaspoon cinnamon or 2 cinnamon sticks
- 1 tablespoon stevia

Directions

1. Add all the ingredients in the instant pot.
2. Secure the lid and turn the pressure release handle to the 'sealed position.
3. Select the 'manual' function, set to high pressure and adjust the timer to 8 minutes.
4. Once it beeps, 'quick release' the steam and remove the lid.
5. Serve when cool, or save in a bottle for later use.

Nutrition Values Per Serving:

Calories: 62

Carbohydrate: 13.7g

Protein: 0.1g

Fat: 0g

Sugar: 11g

Sodium: 2mg

Roasted Tomato Sauce

Serving: 4

Preparation Time: 10 minutes

Cooking Time: 10 minutes

Ingredients

- 1 red onion, chopped
- 1 green bell pepper, chopped
- 1 jalapeño pepper, sliced
- 8 garlic cloves
- 4 chipotle chilies in adobo sauce
- 2 teaspoon powdered cumin
- 4 teaspoons Mexican red chili powder
- 4 teaspoons salt
- 1 cup water
- 28 oz. canned, fire-roasted, diced tomatoes

Directions

1. Add all the ingredients in the instant pot.
2. Secure the lid and turn the pressure release handle to the 'sealed' position.
3. Select the 'manual' function, set to high pressure and adjust the timer to 10 minutes.
4. After the beep, 'quick release' the steam and remove the lid.

5. Transfer the sauce to a blender and blend well to form a smooth mixture
6. Use immediately or save in a bottle for later use.

Nutrition Values Per Serving:

Calories: 96

Carbohydrate: 18.4g

Protein: 3.9g

Fat: 1.4g

Sugar: 7.9g

Sodium: 2109mg

Tomato Basil Sauce

Serving: 8

Preparation Time: 5 minutes

Cooking Time: 15 minutes

Ingredients

- 4 tablespoons olive oil
- ½ garlic cloves, minced
- 2 onions, diced
- 8 lbs Roma tomatoes, diced
- 2 tablespoons salt
- 1 tablespoon pepper
- 1 tablespoon garlic powder
- 3 tablespoons Italian seasoning
- ½ teaspoon crushed peppers
- 2 bay leaves
- 1 cup chopped fresh basil

Directions

1. Add the oil into the instant pot and select the 'sauté' function.
2. Add the garlic and onions to the oil and stir-fry for 5 minutes.
3. Now add all the remaining ingredients, except the basil to the instant pot.

4. Secure the lid and turn the pressure release handle to the 'sealed' position.
5. Select the 'Manual' function, set to high pressure and adjust the timer to 10 minutes.
6. After the beep, 'Quick release' the steam and remove the lid.
7. Stir well, remove the bay leaves and add the basil to the sauce.
8. Serve.

Nutrition Values Per Serving:

Calories: 197

Carbohydrate: 25.2g

Protein: 0.7g

Fat: 8.7g

Sugar: 15.5g

Sodium: 2133 mg

Bolognese Eggplant Sauce

- Serving: 6
- Preparation Time: 10 minutes
- Cooking Time: 35 minutes

Ingredients

- ½ large onion, finely chopped
- 1 carrot, finely chopped
- 1½ celery stalk, finely chopped
- 1½ garlic clove, minced or pressed
- ½ tablespoon olive oil
- ½ (6 oz. can tomato paste
- 1 lb ground beef
- 1 eggplant, diced
- ½ tablespoon salt
- ½ teaspoon black pepper
- ¾ teaspoon dried thyme
- 1 teaspoon dried oregano
- 1 28 oz. can crushed tomatoes
- 1 cup whole milk
- 1 cup dry red wine
- Pasta for serving

Directions

1. Pour the oil into the instant pot. Select the 'sauté' function.
2. Put all the vegetables into the oil and stir-fry for 10 minutes.
3. Stir in the tomato paste and all the spices. Use an immerse blender to blend the sauce.
4. Now put all the remaining ingredients in the instant pot.
5. Secure the lid and turn the pressure release handle to the 'sealed' position.
6. Select the 'manual' function, set to high pressure and adjust the timer to 35 minutes.
7. After the beep, 'quick release' the steam and remove the lid.
8. Stir well and serve with pasta.

Nutrition Values Per Serving:

Calories: 259

Carbohydrate: 14.7g

Protein: 26.5g

Fat: 7.5g

Sugar: 8.8g

Sodium: 716mg

Beets Tomato Sauce

Serving: 4

Preparation Time: 10 minutes

Cooking Time: 10 minutes

Ingredients

- 1 tablespoon olive oil
- ½ large onion, diced
- 2½ ribs of celery, diced
- 4 carrots, diced
- 4 garlic cloves, diced
- ½ cup butternut squash, peeled and cubed
- 2 beets, peeled and diced
- 2 tablespoons fresh lemon juice
- ½ cup broth
- 1 bay leaf
- ½ small bunch fresh basil, roughly chopped
- ¼ teaspoon sea salt

Directions

1. Add the oil into the instant pot. Select the 'sauté' function.
2. Put all the vegetables into the oil and stir-fry for 5 minutes.
3. Stir in all the remaining ingredients.

4. Secure the lid and turn the pressure release handle to the 'Sealed' position.
5. Select the 'Manual' function, set to high pressure and adjust the timer to 10 minutes.
6. Once it beeps, 'Quick release' the steam and remove the lid.
7. Remove the bay leaf then transfer the sauce to a blender and blend well to form a smooth mixture
8. Use immediately or save in a bottle for later use.

Nutrition Values Per Serving:

Calories: 108

Carbohydrate: 16.9g

Protein: 2.8g

Fat: 3.9g

Sugar: 8.8g

Sodium: 316mg

Bolognese Lentil Sauce

Serving: 6

Preparation Time: 15 minutes

Cooking Time: 20 minutes

Ingredients

- ½ large onion, finely chopped
- 1 carrot, finely chopped
- 1½ celery stalks, finely chopped
- 1½ garlic cloves, minced or pressed
- ½ tablespoon olive oil
- ½ can tomato paste (6 oz
- ½ cup lentils, soaked, rinsed and drained
- ½ tablespoon salt
- ½ teaspoon black pepper
- ¾ teaspoon dried thyme
- 1 teaspoon dried oregano
- 1 can crushed tomatoes (28 oz
- 1 cup whole milk
- 1 cup dry red wine
- Pasta for serving

Directions

1. Pour the oil into the instant pot and select the 'sauté' function.

2. Put all the vegetables into the oil and stir-fry for 10 minutes.
3. Stir in the tomato paste and all the spices. Use an immerse blender to blend the sauce.
4. Now put all the remaining ingredients into the instant pot.
5. Secure the lid and turn the pressure release handle to the 'sealed' position.
6. Select the 'manual' function, set to high pressure and adjust the timer to 20 minutes.
7. After the beep, 'quick release' the steam and remove the lid.
8. Stir well and serve with pasta.

Nutrition Values Per Serving:

Calories: 156

Carbohydrate: 19.8g

Protein: 6.9g

Fat: 2.8g

Sugar: 6.8g

Sodium: 666mg

Apple Cinnamon Sauce

Serving: 6

Preparation Time: 10 minutes

Cooking Time: 07 minutes

Ingredients

- 1 lb Fuji apples, unpeeled, quartered
- 1 lb Golden Delicious apples, unpeeled, quartered
- ½ lb Granny Smith apples, unpeeled, quartered
- ½ cup cold water
- 1 teaspoon pure vanilla extract or vanilla bean paste
- ½ tablespoon ground cinnamon
- ⅛ teaspoon ground cardamom
- 1 large pinch kosher salt

Directions

1. Put all the ingredients into the instant pot.
2. Secure the lid and turn the pressure release handle to the 'sealed' position.
3. Select the 'manual' function, set to high pressure and adjust the timer to 7 minutes.
4. After the beep, 'natural release' the steam and remove the lid.
5. Transfer the sauce to a blender and blend well to form a smooth mixture.

6. Use immediately or save in a bottle for later use.

Nutrition Values Per Serving:

Calories: 98

Carbohydrate: 26.2g

Protein: 0.3g

Fat: 0.2g

Sugar: 20g

Sodium: 99mg

Spicy Indian Sauce

Serving: 3

Preparation Time: 10 minutes

Cooking Time: 25 minutes

Ingredients

- 1 tablespoon olive oil
- 1½ large onions, finely diced
- 1½ garlic cloves, finely chopped
- ½ inch knob fresh ginger, peeled and grated
- Sea salt to taste
- ½ tablespoon ground coriander
- ½ tablespoon ground cumin
- ¼ teaspoon cayenne pepper
- ½ teaspoon ground turmeric
- ½ tablespoon sweet paprika
- ½ (28 oz. can whole tomatoes

½ cup water

Directions

1. Add the oil and then onions, garlic, and ginger into the instant pot and select the 'sauté' function and stir-fry for 5 minutes.
2. Now add all the vegetables into the pot and stir-fry for another 5 minutes.

3. Add all the remaining ingredients to the instant pot.
4. Secure the lid and turn the pressure release handle to the 'sealed' position.
5. Select the 'manual' function, set to high pressure and adjust the timer to 15 minutes.
6. After the beep, 'quick release' the steam and remove the lid.
7. Stir well and serve.

Nutrition Values Per Serving:

Calories: 83

Carbohydrate: 9.8g

Protein: 1.6g

Fat: 3.9g

Sugar: 2.5g

Sodium: 181mg

Instant Marinara Sauce

Serving: 5

Preparation Time: 10 minutes

Cooking Time: 16 minutes

Ingredients

- 4 tablespoons olive oil
- 2 small onions, chopped
- 2 cloves garlic, minced
- 2 carrots, diced
- 4 cans tomatoes, diced
- 3 teaspoons dried basil
- 3 teaspoons dried oregano
- 1½ teaspoons sea salt
- Freshly ground black pepper to taste
- 2 tablespoons butter, unsalted
- Fresh Parsley, chopped

Directions

1. Add the oil into the instant pot and 'select the 'sauté' function.
2. Put all the vegetables into the oil and stir-fry for 5 minutes.
3. Now put all the remaining ingredients, except the butter and black pepper, into the instant pot.

4. Secure the lid and turn the pressure release handle to the 'sealed' position.
5. Select the 'manual' function, set to high pressure and adjust the timer to 10 minutes.
6. After the beep, 'quick release' the steam and remove the lid.
7. Use an immerse blender to blend the sauce into a smooth paste.
8. Add the butter and black pepper, and cook for 1 minute on the 'sauté' function.
9. Stir well and serve.

Nutrition Values Per Serving:

Calories: 148

Carbohydrate: 6.1g

Protein: 0.9g

Fat: 13.3g

Sugar: 3.1g

Potato and Shrimp Salad

Preparation time: 10 minutes

Cooking time: 16 minutes

Servings: 4

Ingredients:

- 1 pound baby red potatoes, peeled and halved
- 1 red onion, chopped
- 1 pound shrimp, peeled and deveined
- 1 tablespoon olive oil
- 1 teaspoon hot paprika
- 1 tablespoon basil, chopped
- A pinch of salt and black pepper
- 1 tablespoon chives, chopped
- 1 cup veggie stock
- 1 teaspoon lemon juice

Directions:

- Set your instant pot on Sauté mode, add the oil, heat it up, add the onion and sauté for 2 minutes.
- Add the potatoes and the rest of the ingredients except the shrimp and chives, put the lid on and cook on High for 10 minutes.
- Release the pressure naturally for 10 minutes, set the pot on Sauté mode, add the chives and shrimp, cook for 4 minutes more, divide into small bowls and serve cold as an appetizer.

Nutritional Values per serving: Calories 201, fat 9, fiber 4, carbs 7, protein 10

Cheesy Artichokes Spread

Preparation time: 10 minutes

Cooking time: 8 minutes

Servings: 8

Ingredients:

- 20 ounces canned artichoke hearts, drained
- 8 ounces cream cheese, soft
- 14 ounces cheddar cheese, grated
- ½ cup chicken stock
- ½ cup coconut cream
- A pinch of salt and black pepper
- 3 garlic cloves, minced
- 1 teaspoon chili powder

Directions:

In your instant pot, combine the artichokes with the stock, garlic, chili powder, salt and pepper, put the lid on and cook on High for 8 minutes.

Release the pressure naturally for 10 minutes, transfer the mix to a food processor, add the remaining ingredients, blend well, divide into bowls and serve.

Nutritional Values per serving: Calories 200, fat 8, fiber 2, carbs 6, protein 8

Endives Platter

Preparation time: 5 minutes

Cooking time: 12 minutes

Servings: 4

Ingredients:

- 4 endives, halved
- 1 cup water
- A pinch of salt and black pepper
- 2 garlic cloves, chopped
- ¼ cup olive oil
- 2 tablespoons lemon juice
- 3 garlic cloves

Directions:

- Add water to the instant pot, add the steamer basket inside, arrange the endives in the pot, put the lid on and cook on High for 12 minutes.
- Release the pressure fast for 5 minutes, transfer the endives to a bowl, add the rest of the ingredients, toss, arrange them on a platter and serve.

Nutritional Values per serving: Calories 171, fat 3, fiber 4, carbs 7, protein 5

Crunchy Mushrooms

Preparation Time: 10 minutes

Servings 4

Nutritional Values per serving: 91 Calories; 6.4g Fat; 5.5g Total Carbs; 5.2g Protein; 2.8g Sugars

Ingredients

- 2 tablespoons butter, melted
- 20 ounces button mushrooms, brushed clean
- 2 cloves garlic, minced
- 1 teaspoon dried basil
- 1 teaspoon dried rosemary
- 1 teaspoon dried sage
- 1 bay leaf
- Sea salt, to taste
- 1/2 teaspoon freshly ground black pepper
- 1/2 cup water
- 1/2 cup broth, preferably homemade
- 1 tablespoon soy sauce
- 1 tablespoon fresh parsley leaves, roughly chopped

Directions

1. Press the "Sauté" button to heat up your Instant Pot. Once hot, melt the butter and sauté the mushrooms and garlic until aromatic.

2. Add seasonings, water, and broth. Add garlic, oregano, mushrooms, thyme, basil, bay leaves, veggie broth, and salt and pepper to your instant pot.
3. Secure the lid. Choose "Manual" mode and High pressure; cook for 5 minutes. Once cooking is complete, use a quick pressure release; carefully remove the lid.
4. Arrange your mushrooms on a serving platter and serve with cocktail sticks. Bon appétit!

Wrapped Shrimp

Preparation time: 5 minutes

Cooking time: 6 minutes

Servings: 4

Ingredients:

1 pound shrimp, peeled and deveined

1 cup tomato sauce

A drizzle of olive oil

8 ounces bacon slices

1 teaspoon chili powder

A pinch of salt and black pepper

Directions:

1. In a bowl, mix the shrimp with the oil, salt, pepper and chili powder and toss.
2. Set the instant pot on Sauté mode, add the shrimp and cook for 2 minutes.
3. Transfer the shrimp to a bowl, cool it down and wrap each in a bacon slice.
4. Put the tomato sauce in your instant pot, arrange wrapper shrimp inside, put the lid on and cook on High for 4 minutes.
5. Release the pressure fast for 5 minutes, arrange the shrimp on a platter and serve.

Nutritional Values per serving: Calories 162, fat 3, fiber 4, carbs 7, protein 6

Lentils Spread

Preparation time: 10 minutes

Cooking time: 20 minutes

Servings: 6

Ingredients:

- 20 ounces tomatoes, crushed
- 3 garlic cloves, minced
- 1 and ½ cups red lentils, rinsed
- A pinch of salt and black pepper
- 1 tablespoon chives, chopped
- 1 tablespoon lemon juice
- 1 and ½ cups low-sodium veggie stock

Directions:

1. In your instant pot, mix the tomatoes with the lentils, salt, pepper and the stock, put the lid on and cook on High for 20 minutes.
2. Release the pressure naturally for 10 minutes, transfer the lentils mix to a food processor, add the rest of the ingredients except the chives, pulse well, divide into small bowls, sprinkle the chives on top and serve.

Nutritional Values per serving: Calories 167, fat 4, fiber 3, carbs 8, protein 6

Paprika Cranberry Dip

Preparation time: 6 minutes

Cooking time: 15 minutes

Servings: 4

Ingredients:

- 2 and ½ teaspoons lemon zest, grated
- 1 teaspoon chili powder
- 1 teaspoon sweet paprika
- 12 ounces cranberries
- ¼ cup orange juice

Directions:

1. In your instant pot, combine all the ingredients, put the lid on and cook on High for 15 minutes.
2. Release the pressure fast for 6 minutes, blend the mix using an immersion blender, divide into bowls and serve as a dip.

Nutritional Values per serving: Calories 141, fat 2, fiber 4, carbs 5, protein 4

Citrus Onion Spread

Preparation time: 5 minutes

Cooking time: 7 minutes.

Servings: 4

Ingredients:

- 1 cup cream cheese, soft
- A pinch of salt and black pepper
- 1 tablespoon olive oil
- 6 spring onions, chopped
- Juice of 1 orange
- 1 cup water

Directions:

1. In a bowl, combine the cream cheese with spring onions and the rest of the ingredients except the water, whisk well and transfer to a ramekin.
2. Add the water in the instant pot, add the trivet inside, place the ramekin in the pot, put the lid on and cook on Low for 7 minutes.
3. Release the pressure fast for 5 minutes and serve the spread right away.

Nutritional Values per serving: Calories 120, fat 2, fiber 3, carbs 5, protein 4

Zucchini and Squash Dip

Preparation time: 5 minutes

Cooking time: 15 minutes

Servings: 4

Ingredients:

- 1 yellow onion, chopped
- 1 tablespoon olive oil
- 1 and ½ pounds zucchini, chopped
- 1 butternut squash, peeled and roughly chopped
- ½ cup veggie stock
- 1 tablespoon lemon juice
- 1 tablespoon basil, chopped
- 2 garlic cloves, minced
- 1 tablespoon mint, chopped

Directions:

1. Set your instant pot on Sauté mode, add the oil, heat it up, add the onion and garlic, stir and cook 4 minutes.
2. Add zucchinis and the rest of the ingredients except the basil and the mint, put the lid on and cook on High for 10 minutes.
3. Release the pressure fast for 5 minutes, blend the mix using an immersion blender, divide into bowls and serve with mint and basil sprinkled on top.

Nutritional Values per serving: Calories 170, fat 5, fiber 3, carbs 4, protein 6

Garlic Cauliflower Dip

Preparation time: 10 minutes

Cooking time: 15 minutes

Servings: 4

Ingredients:

- 1 yellow onion, chopped
- 1 tablespoon olive oil
- A pinch of salt and black pepper
- 1 tablespoon rosemary, chopped
- 3 garlic cloves, minced
- ½ cup chicken stock
- 1 pound cauliflower florets
- ½ cup coconut cream
- 1 tablespoons parsley, chopped

Directions:

1. Set your instant pot on Sauté mode, add the oil, heat it up, add the onion, stir and cook for 5 minutes.
2. Add the rest of the ingredients except the cream and parsley, put the lid on and cook on High for 10 minutes.
3. Release the pressure naturally for 10 minutes, add the cream, blend the mix using an immersion blender, divide into bowls, sprinkle the parsley on top and serve as a party dip.

Nutritional Values per serving: Calories 170, fat 3, fiber 2, carbs 6, protein 7

Broccoli Spread

Preparation time: 10 minutes

Cooking time: 12 minutes

Servings: 4

Ingredients:

- 2 tablespoons avocado oil
- 8 garlic cloves, minced
- ½ cup veggie stock
- 6 cups broccoli florets
- A pinch of salt and black pepper
- 3 tablespoons cream cheese, soft

Directions:

1. Set your instant pot on Sauté mode, add the oil, heat it up, add the garlic and brown for 2 minutes.
2. Add the rest of the ingredients except the cream cheese, put the lid on and cook on Low for 10 minutes.
3. Release the pressure naturally for 10 minutes, transfer the broccoli mix to a blender, add the cream cheese, pulse well, divide into bowls and serve as a party spread.

Nutritional Values per serving: Calories 178, fat 3, fiber 3, carbs 5, protein 8

Cumin Cheese Spread

Preparation time: 5 minutes

Cooking time: 8 minutes

Servings: 4

Ingredients:

- 1 teaspoon olive oil
- 1 red onion, chopped
- 2 spring onions, chopped
- 1 cup cream cheese, soft
- 2 teaspoons cumin, ground
- ¼ teaspoon red pepper flakes
- A pinch of salt and black pepper
- 1 cup water

Directions:

1. In a bowl, combine the cream cheese with spring onions and the rest of the ingredients except the water, whisk really well and put everything in a ramekin.
2. Add the water to your instant pot, add the trivet and put the ramekin inside.
3. Put the lid on, cook on Low for 8 minutes, release the pressure fast for 5 minutes and serve the spread right away.

Nutritional Values per serving: Calories 170, fat 2, fiber 3, carbs 6, protein 8

Leeks and Bell Pepper Spread

Preparation time: 10 minutes

Cooking time: 15 minutes

Servings: 6

Ingredients:

- ¼ cup veggie stock
- 1 pound red bell peppers, chopped
- 4 leeks, sliced
- A pinch of salt and black pepper
- 1 tablespoon olive oil
- 1 tablespoon lemon juice
- 2 tablespoons cream cheese
- 2 garlic cloves, minced
- 1 tablespoon cilantro, chopped

Directions:

1. In your instant pot, combine the bell peppers with the leeks and the rest of the ingredients except the cream cheese and cilantro, put the lid on and cook on High for 15 minutes.
2. Release the pressure naturally for 10 minutes, transfer the mix to a blender, add the cream cheese and pulse well.
3. Divide into bowls and serve as a spread with the cilantro sprinkled on top.

Nutritional Values per serving: Calories 180, fat 4, fiber 3, carbs 7, protein 9

Chicken, Spinach and Avocado Salad

Preparation time: 10 minutes

Cooking time: 15 minutes

Servings: 4

Ingredients:

- 1 avocado, pitted, peeled and cubed
- 2 tablespoons Greek yogurt
- 2 tablespoons mayonnaise
- 2 spring onions, chopped
- 1 and ½ cups baby spinach
- 1 cup chicken stock
- A pinch of salt and black pepper
- 1 pound chicken breast, skinless, boneless and cubed

Directions:

1. In your instant pot, combine the chicken with salt, pepper and the stock, put the lid on and cook on High for 15 minutes.
2. Release the pressure naturally for 10 minutes, drain the chicken, transfer it to a bowl, add the rest of the ingredients, toss, divide into small bowls and serve as an appetizer.

Nutritional Values per serving: Calories 224, fat 12, fiber 4, carbs 7, protein 12

Pesto Barley Bowls

Preparation time: 5 minutes

Cooking time: 20 minutes

Servings: 4

Ingredients:

- 1 cup hulled barley, rinsed
- 2 cups veggie stock
- ¾ cup basil pesto
- 1 tablespoon chives, chopped
- 1 red onion, chopped
- 1 celery stalks chopped
- A pinch of salt and black pepper

Directions:

1. In your instant pot, combine the barley with the stock, salt and pepper, toss, put the lid on and cook on High for 20 minutes.
2. Release the pressure fast for 5 minutes, stir the barley, transfer to a bowl, add the rest of the ingredients and toss well.
3. Divide into cups and serve as an appetizer.

Nutritional Values per serving: Calories 172, fat 4, fiber 4, carbs 7, protein 9

Balsamic Olives Salsa

Preparation time: 5 minutes

Cooking time: 5 minutes

Servings: 4

Ingredients:

- 1 tablespoon balsamic vinegar
- 1 tablespoon olive oil
- 1 cup cherry tomatoes, halved
- 2 green onions, chopped
- 2 cups kalamata olives, pitted and chopped
- 1 handful basil leaves, chopped
- 1 handful parsley leaves, chopped

Directions:

1. Set your instant pot on Sauté mode, add the oil, heat it up, add the tomatoes and the rest of the ingredients, toss, put the lid on and cook on High for 5 minutes.
2. Release the pressure fast for 5 minutes, divide the salsa into bowls and serve cold as an appetizer.

Nutritional Values per serving: Calories 152, fat 2, fiber 3, carbs 6, protein 7

Cheese Dip with Peppers

Preparation Time: 10 minutes

Servings 8

Nutritional Values per serving: 237 Calories; 20.6g Fat; 3.1g Total Carbs; 10.2g Protein; 1.8g Sugars

Ingredients

- 1 tablespoon butter
- 2 red bell peppers, sliced
- 1 teaspoon red Aleppo pepper flakes
- 1 cup cream cheese, room temperature
- 2 cups Colby cheese, shredded
- 1 teaspoon sumac
- 2 garlic cloves, minced
- 1 cup chicken broth
- Salt and ground black pepper, to taste

Directions

1. Press the "Sauté" button to heat up your Instant Pot. Once hot, melt the butter. Sauté the peppers until just tender.
2. Add the remaining ingredients; gently stir to combine.
3. Secure the lid. Choose "Manual" mode and High pressure; cook for 3 minutes. Once cooking is complete, use a quick pressure release; carefully remove the lid.
4. Serve with your favorite keto dippers. Bon appétit!

Juicy Chicken Drumettes

Preparation Time: 15 minutes

Servings 8

Nutritional Values per serving: 237 Calories; 20.6g Fat; 3.1g Total Carbs; 10.2g Protein; 1.8g Sugars

Ingredients

- 2 pounds chicken drumettes
- 1 stick butter
- 1 tablespoon coconut aminos
- Sea salt and ground black pepper, to taste
- 1/2 teaspoon dried dill weed
- 1/2 teaspoon dried basil
- 1 teaspoon hot sauce
- 1 tablespoon fish sauce
- 1/2 cup tomato sauce
- 1/2 cup water

Directions

1. Add all ingredients to your Instant Pot.
2. Secure the lid. Choose "Poultry" mode and High pressure; cook for 10 minutes. Once cooking is complete, use a natural pressure release; carefully remove the lid.
3. Serve at room temperature and enjoy!

Creamy Cauliflower Bites

Preparation Time: 25 minutes

Servings 8

Nutritional Values per serving: 157 Calories; 12.1g Fat; 3.6g Total Carbs; 8.9g Protein; 1.2g Sugars

Ingredients

- 1 head of cauliflower, broken into florets
- 2 tablespoons butter
- Coarse sea salt and white pepper, to taste
- 1/2 teaspoon cayenne pepper
- 1 garlic clove, minced
- 1/2 cup Parmesan cheese, grated
- 1 cup Asiago cheese, shredded
- 2 tablespoons fresh chopped chives, minced
- 2 eggs, beaten

Directions

1. Add 1 cup of water and a steamer basket to the Instant Pot. Now, add cauliflower to the steamer basket.
2. Secure the lid. Choose "Manual" mode and High pressure; cook for 3 minutes. Once cooking is complete, use a quick pressure release; carefully remove the lid.
3. Transfer the cauliflower to a food processor. Add the remaining ingredients; process until everything is well incorporated.
4. Shape the mixture into balls. Bake in the preheated oven at 400 degrees F for 18 minutes. Bon appétit!

Yummy Baby Carrots

Preparation Time: 10 minutes

Servings 8

Nutritional Values per serving: 94 Calories; 6.1g Fat; 5.9g Total Carbs; 1.4g Protein; 3.1g Sugars

Ingredients

- 28 ounces baby carrots
- 1 cup chicken broth
- 1/2 cup water
- 1/2 stick butter
- 2 tablespoons balsamic vinegar
- Coarse sea salt, to taste
- 1/2 teaspoon red pepper flakes, crushed
- 1/2 teaspoon dried dill weed

Directions

1. Simply add all of the above ingredients to your Instant Pot.
2. Secure the lid. Choose "Manual" mode and High pressure; cook for 3 minutes. Once cooking is complete, use a quick pressure release; carefully remove the lid.
3. Transfer to a nice serving bowl and serve. Enjoy!

Cheesy Keto Dip

Preparation Time: 10 minutes

Servings 10

Nutritional Values per serving: 280 Calories; 20.4g Fat; 3.7g Total Carbs; 20.6g Protein; 2.5g Sugars

Ingredients

- 10 ounces cream cheese
- 10 ounces Pepper-Jack cheese
- 1 pound tomatoes, pureed
- 10 ounces pancetta, chopped
- 1 cup green olives, pitted and halved
- 1/2 teaspoon garlic powder
- 1 teaspoon dried oregano
- 1 cup chicken broth
- 4 ounces Mozzarella cheese, thinly sliced

Directions

1. Combine cream cheese, Pepper-Jack cheese, tomatoes, pancetta, olives, garlic, powder, and oregano in your Instant Pot.
2. Secure the lid. Choose "Manual" mode and High pressure; cook for 4 minutes. Once cooking is complete, use a quick pressure release; carefully remove the lid.
3. Top with Mozzarella cheese; cover and let it sit in the residual heat. Serve warm or at room temperature. Bon appétit!

Simple Brussels Sprouts

Preparation Time: 10 minutes

Servings 4

Nutritional Values per serving: 68 Calories; 3.3g Fat; 5.8g Total Carbs; 3.5g Protein; 1.9g Sugars

Ingredients

- 1 tablespoon butter
- 1/2 cup shallots, chopped
- 3/4 pound whole Brussels sprouts
- Sea salt, to taste
- 1/4 teaspoon ground black pepper
- 1/2 cup water
- 1/2 cup chicken stock

Directions

1. Press the "Sauté" button to heat up your Instant Pot. Once hot, melt the butter and sauté the shallots until tender and translucent.
2. Add the remaining ingredients to the Instant Pot.
3. Secure the lid. Choose "Manual" mode and High pressure; cook for 4 minutes. Once cooking is complete, use a quick pressure release; carefully remove the lid.
4. Transfer Brussels sprouts to a serving platter. Serve with cocktail sticks and enjoy!

Quick Spinach Dip

Preparation Time: 5 minutes

Servings 10

Nutritional Values per serving: 43 Calories; 1.7g Fat; 3.5g Total Carbs; 4.1g Protein; 1.3g Sugars

Ingredients

- 1 pound spinach
- 4 ounces Cottage cheese, at room temperature
- 4 ounces Cheddar cheese, grated
- 1 teaspoon garlic powder
- 1/2 teaspoon shallot powder
- 1/2 teaspoon celery seeds
- 1/2 teaspoon fennel seeds
- 1/2 teaspoon cayenne pepper
- Salt and black pepper, to taste

Directions

1. Add all of the above ingredients to your Instant Pot.
2. Serve warm or at room temperature. Bon appétit!
3. Secure the lid. Choose "Manual" mode and High pressure; cook for 1 minute. Once cooking is complete, use a quick pressure release; carefully remove the lid.

Asparagus with Mayo Dip

Preparation Time: 5 minutes

Servings 6

Nutritional Values per serving: 116 Calories; 8.5g Fat; 6.9g Total Carbs; 4.5g Protein; 2.4g Sugars

Ingredients

- 1 ½ pounds asparagus spears, trimmed
- 1/2 cup sour cream
- 1/2 cup mayonnaise
- 2 tablespoons fresh chervil
- 2 tablespoons scallions, chopped
- 1 teaspoon garlic, minced
- Salt, to taste

Directions

- Add 1 cup of water and a steamer basket to you Instant Pot.
- Secure the lid. Choose "Manual" mode and High pressure; cook for 1 minute. Once cooking is complete, use a quick pressure release; carefully remove the lid.
- Then, thoroughly combine the remaining ingredients to make your dipping sauce. Serve your asparagus with the dipping sauce on the side. Bon appétit!

Keto Greens Dip

Preparation Time: 10 minutes

Servings 10

Nutritional Values per serving: 153 Calories; 10.6g Fat; 5g Total Carbs; 8.7g Protein; 3.1g Sugars

Ingredients

- 2 tablespoons butter, melted
- 20 ounces mustard greens
- 2 bell peppers, chopped
- 1 white onion, chopped
- 1 teaspoon garlic, minced
- Sea salt and ground black pepper, to taste
- 1 cup chicken stock
- 8 ounces Neufchâtel cheese, crumbled
- 1/2 teaspoon dried thyme
- 1/2 teaspoon dried dill
- 1/2 teaspoon turmeric powder
- 3/4 cup Romano cheese, preferably freshly grated

Directions

1. Add the butter, mustard greens, bell peppers, onion, and garlic to the Instant Pot.
2. Secure the lid. Choose "Manual" mode and High pressure; cook for 3 minutes. Once cooking is complete, use a quick pressure release; carefully remove the lid.
3. Then, add the remaining ingredients and press the "Sauté" button. Let it simmer until the cheese is melted; then, gently stir this mixture until everything is well incorporated.
4. Serve with your favorite low-carb dippers.

Cocktail Sausages Asian-Style

Preparation Time: 10 minutes

Servings 8

Nutritional Values per serving: 330 Calories; 24.8g Fat; 2.7g Total Carbs; 22.7g Protein; 1.2g Sugars

Ingredients

- 1 teaspoon sesame oil
- 20 mini cocktail sausages
- 1/2 cup tomato puree
- 1/2 cup chicken stock
- 1 tablespoon dark soy sauce
- 1/3 teaspoon ground black pepper
- 1/2 teaspoon paprika
- Himalayan salt, to taste
- 1/2 teaspoon mustard seeds
- 1/2 teaspoon fennel seeds
- 1/4 teaspoon fresh ginger root, peeled and grated
- 1 teaspoon garlic paste

Directions

1. Simply throw all ingredients into your Instant Pot.
2. Secure the lid. Choose "Manual" mode and High pressure; cook for 4 minutes. Once cooking is complete, use a quick pressure release; carefully remove the lid.
3. Serve with cocktail sticks and enjoy!

Stuffed Mushrooms with Cheese

Preparation Time: 10 minutes

Servings 5

Nutritional Values per serving: 151 Calories; 9.2g Fat; 6g Total Carbs; 11.9g Protein; 3.6g Sugars

Ingredients

- 1 tablespoon butter, softened
- 1 shallot, chopped
- 2 cloves garlic, minced
- 1 ½ cups Cottage cheese, at room temperature
- 1/2 cup Romano cheese, grated
- 1 red bell pepper, chopped
- 1 green bell pepper, chopped
- 1 jalapeno pepper, minced
- 1/2 teaspoon dried basil
- 1/2 teaspoon dried oregano
- 1/2 teaspoon dried rosemary
- 10 medium-sized button mushrooms, stems removed

Directions

1. Press the "Sauté" button to heat up your Instant Pot. Once hot, melt the butter and sauté the shallots until tender and translucent.
2. Stir in the garlic and cook an additional 30 seconds or until aromatic. Now, add the remaining ingredients, except for the mushroom caps, and stir to combine well.
3. Then, fill the mushroom caps with this mixture.
4. Add 1 cup of water and a steamer basket to you Instant Pot. Arrange the stuffed mushrooms in the steamer basket.
5. Secure the lid. Choose "Manual" mode and High pressure; cook for 5 minutes. Once cooking is complete, use a quick pressure release; carefully remove the lid.
6. Arrange the stuffed mushroom on a serving platter and serve. Enjoy!

Family Meatballs

Preparation Time: 15 minutes

Servings 6

Nutritional Values per serving: 384 Calories; 22.2g Fat; 6.1g Total Carbs; 38.4g Protein; 3.6g Sugars

Ingredients

- 1/2 pound ground pork
- 1 pound ground beef
- 1/2 cup Romano cheese, grated
- 1/2 cup pork rinds, crushed
- 1 egg, beaten
- Coarse sea salt and ground black pepper, to taste
- 1 teaspoon granulated garlic
- 1/2 teaspoon cayenne pepper
- 1/2 teaspoon dried basil
- 1/4 cup milk, lukewarm
- 1 ½ cups BBQ sauce

Directions

1. Thoroughly combine ground meat, cheese, pork rinds, egg, salt, black pepper, garlic, cayenne pepper, basil, and milk in the mixing bowl.
2. Then, roll the mixture into 20 meatballs.
3. Pour BBQ sauce into your Instant Pot. Now, add the meatballs and secure the lid.
4. Choose "Manual" mode and High pressure; cook for 8 minutes. Once cooking is complete, use a quick pressure release; carefully remove the lid. Bon appétit!

Fresh Keto Meatballs

Preparation Time: 15 minutes

Servings 6

Nutritional Values per serving: 280 Calories; 20.4g Fat; 3.7g Total Carbs; 20.6g Protein; 2.5g Sugars

Ingredients

- 1/2 pound ground pork
- 1/2 pound ground turkey
- 2 eggs
- 1/3 cup almond flour
- Sea salt and ground black pepper, to taste
- 2 garlic cloves, minced
- 1 cup Romano cheese, grated
- 1 teaspoon dried basil
- 1/2 teaspoon dried thyme
- 1/4 cup minced fresh mint, plus more for garnish
- 1/2 cup beef bone broth
- 1/2 cup tomatoes, puréed
- 2 tablespoons scallions

Directions

1. Thoroughly combine all ingredients, except for broth, tomatoes, and scallions in a mixing bowl.
2. Shape the mixture into 2-inch meatballs and reserve.
3. Add beef bone broth, tomatoes, and scallions to your Instant Pot. Place the meatballs in this sauce.
4. Secure the lid. Choose "Manual" mode and High pressure; cook for 8 minutes. Once cooking is complete, use a quick pressure release; carefully remove the lid. Bon appétit!
5. Parmigiano Chicken Wings

Preparation Time: 20 minutes

Servings 12

Nutritional Values per serving: 443 Calories; 30.8g Fat; 6.2g Total Carbs; 33.2g Protein; 3.5g Sugars

Ingredients

- 4 pounds chicken wings cut into sections
- 1/2 cup butter, melted
- 1 tablespoon Italian seasoning mix
- 1/2 teaspoon onion powder
- 1/2 teaspoon garlic powder
- 1 teaspoon paprika
- 1/2 teaspoon coarse sea salt
- 1/2 teaspoon ground black pepper
- 1 cup Parmigiano-Reggiano cheese, shaved
- 2 eggs, lightly whisked

Directions

1. Add chicken wings, butter, Italian seasoning mix, onion powder, garlic powder, paprika, salt, and black pepperto your Instant Pot.
2. Secure the lid. Choose "Poultry" mode and High pressure. Cook the chicken wings for 10 minutes. Once cooking is complete, use a natural pressure release; carefully remove the lid.
3. Mix Parmigiano-Reggiano cheese with eggs. Spoon this mixture over the wings.
4. Secure the lid. Choose "Manual" mode and High pressure; cook for 4 minutes longer. Once cooking is complete, use a quick pressure release; carefully remove the lid. Bon appétit!

Delicious Cauliflower Tots

Preparation Time: 25 minutes

Servings 6

Nutritional Values per serving: 132 Calories; 8.7g Fat; 4.5g Total Carbs; 9.2g Protein; 1.3g Sugars

Ingredients

- 1 head of cauliflower, broken into florets
- 2 eggs, beaten
- 1 shallot, peeled and chopped
- 1/2 cup Swiss cheese, grated
- 1/2 cup Parmesan cheese, grated
- 2 tablespoons fresh coriander, chopped
- Sea salt and ground black pepper, to taste

Directions

1. Start by adding 1 cup of water and a steamer basket to your Instant Pot.
2. Arrange the cauliflower florets in the steamer basket.
3. Secure the lid. Choose "Manual" mode and High pressure; cook for 3 minutes. Once cooking is complete, use a quick pressure release; carefully remove the lid.
4. Mash the cauliflower and add the remaining ingredients. Form the mixture into a tater-tot shape with oiled hands.
5. Place cauliflower tots on a lightly greased baking sheet. Bake in the preheated oven at 390 degrees F approximately 20 minutes; make sure to flip them halfway through the cooking time.
6. Serve at room temperature. Bon appétit!

Keto Broccoli Balls

Preparation Time: 25 minutes

Servings 8

Nutritional Values per serving: 137 Calories; 9.5g Fat; 4.8g Total Carbs; 8.9g Protein; 1.5g Sugars

Ingredients

- 1 head broccoli, broken into florets
- 1/2 cup Añejo cheese, shredded
- 1 ½ cups Cotija cheese, crumbled
- 3 ounces Ricotta cheese, cut into small chunks
- 1 teaspoon chili pepper flakes

Directions

1. Add 1 cup of water and a steamer basket to the Instant Pot.
2. Place broccoli florets in the steamer basket.
3. Secure the lid. Choose "Manual" mode and Low pressure; cook for 5 minutes. Once cooking is complete, use a quick pressure release; carefully remove the lid.
4. Add the broccoli florets along with the remaining ingredients to your food processor. Process until everything is well incorporated.
5. Shape the mixture into balls and place your balls on a parchment-lined baking sheet. Bake in the preheated oven at 390 degrees F for 15 minutes. Bon appétit!

Cheesy Taco Dip

Preparation Time: 10 minutes

Servings 12

Nutritional Values per serving: 275 Calories; 23.7g Fat; 2.6g Total Carbs; 12.4g Protein; 1.2g Sugars

Ingredients

- 2 teaspoons sesame oil
- 1/2 cup yellow onion, chopped
- 1 pound ground turkey
- 1 teaspoon roasted garlic paste
- 1 teaspoon ancho chili powder
- 1/2 teaspoon dried basil
- 1/2 teaspoon dried Mexican oregano
- 1/4 teaspoon freshly ground black pepper, or more to taste
- Sea salt, to taste
- 10 ounces Ricotta cheese, at room temperature
- 1 cup Mexican cheese, shredded
- 1 cup broth, preferably homemade
- 2 ripe tomatoes, chopped
- 1/3 cup salsa verde

Directions

1. Press the "Sauté" button to heat up your Instant Pot. Once hot, heat the sesame oil; now, sauté the onion until translucent.
2. Stir in ground turkey and continue to sauté until it is no longer pink. Add the remaining ingredients and stir until everything is combined well.
3. Secure the lid. Choose "Manual" mode and High pressure; cook for 6 minutes. Once cooking is complete, use a natural pressure release; carefully remove the lid. Bon appétit!

Meatballs with Cheese

Preparation Time: 15 minutes

Servings 8

Nutritional Values per serving: 277 Calories; 17.4g Fat; 3.1g Total Carbs; 25.8g Protein; 0.9g Sugars

Ingredients

- 1 pound ground beef
- 1/2 cup pork chicharron, crushed
- 1/2 cup Parmesan cheese, grated
- 2 eggs, beaten
- 2 tablespoons fresh scallions, chopped
- 2 tablespoons fresh cilantro, chopped
- 1 teaspoon garlic, minced
- Sea salt, to your liking
- 1/2 teaspoon ground black pepper
- 1/2 teaspoon cayenne pepper
- 1 cup Colby cheese, cubed
- 2 teaspoons olive oil
- 1/2 cup chicken broth
- 1/2 cup BBQ sauce

Directions

1. In a mixing dish, thoroughly combine ground beef, pork chicharron, Parmesan cheese, eggs, scallions, cilantro, garlic, salt, black pepper, and cayenne pepper; mix until everything is well incorporated.
2. Now, shape the mixture into balls. Press one cheese cube into center of each meatball, sealing it inside.
3. Press the "Sauté" button and heat the olive oil. Sear the meatballs for a couple of minutes or until browned on all sides. Pour in chicken broth and BBQ sauce.
4. Secure the lid. Choose the "Manual" setting and cook for 8 minutes under High pressure. Once cooking is complete, use a quick pressure release; carefully remove the lid.
5. Serve your meatballs with the sauce. Bon appétit!

Spanish Fat Bombs

Preparation Time: 10 minutes

Servings 8

Nutritional Values per serving: 307 Calories; 26.8g Fat; 5.1g Total Carbs; 10.9g Protein; 2.9g Sugars

Ingredients

- 1 tablespoon tallow, melted
- 1 yellow onion, chopped
- 1 pound Chorizo sausage
- 1 garlic clove, minced
- 1 red bell pepper, chopped
- 1 cup chicken broth
- 1/2 teaspoon deli mustard
- 1 plum tomato, puréed
- 10 ounces Halloumi cheese, crumbled
- 1/3 cup mayonnaise

Directions

1. Press the "Sauté" button and melt the tallow. Once hot, cook the onion until tender and translucent.
2. Add Chorizo and garlic to your Instant Pot; cook until the sausage is no longer pink; crumble the sausage with a fork.
3. Now, stir in bell pepper, broth, mustard, and tomato.
4. Secure the lid. Choose "Manual" mode and High pressure; cook for 4 minutes. Once cooking is complete, use a quick pressure release; carefully remove the lid.
5. Add the cheese and mayo. Shape the mixture into 2-inch balls and serve. Bon appétit!

Yummy Cocktail Wieners

Preparation Time: 10 minutes

Servings 10

Nutritional Values per serving: 257 Calories; 22.7g Fat; 1.4g Total Carbs; 10.8g Protein; 0.2g Sugars

Ingredients

- 1 pound cocktail wieners
- 1/2 pound sliced bacon, cold cut into slices
- 1/2 cup chicken broth
- 1/2 cup water
- 1/4 cup low-carb ketchup
- 2 tablespoons apple cider vinegar
- 1 tablespoon onion powder
- 1 tablespoon ground mustard
- Salt and pepper to taste

Directions

1. Wrap each cocktail wiener with a slice of bacon; secure with a toothpick.
2. Then, place one layer of bacon wrapped cocktail wieners in the bottom of the Instant Pot. Repeat layering until you run out of the cocktail wieners.
3. In a mixing bowl, thoroughly combine the remaining ingredients. Pour this mixture over the bacon wrapped cocktail wieners.
4. Secure the lid. Choose "Manual" mode and Low pressure; cook for 3 minutes. Once cooking is complete, use a natural pressure release; carefully remove the lid. Enjoy!

Fresh Brussels Sprouts with Aioli Sauce

Preparation Time: 10 minutes

Servings 4

Nutritional Values per serving: 161 Calories; 13.4g Fat; 6g Total Carbs; 3.1g Protein; 2.5g Sugars

Ingredients

- 1 tablespoon butter
- 1/2 cup scallions, chopped
- 3/4 pound Brussels sprouts
- Aioli Sauce:
- 1/4 cup mayonnaise
- 1 garlic clove, minced
- 1 tablespoon fresh lemon juice
- 1/2 teaspoon Dijon mustard

Directions

1. Press the "Sauté" button and melt the butter. Once hot, cook the scallions until softened. Now, add Brussels sprouts and sauté them for 1 minute more.
2. Secure the lid. Choose "Manual" mode and High pressure; cook for 4 minutes. Once cooking is complete, use a quick pressure release; carefully remove the lid.
3. Meanwhile, mix mayonnaise, garlic, lemon juice, Dijon mustard. Serve Brussels sprouts with Aioli sauce on the side. Bon appétit!

Cheesy Bacon Bites

Preparation Time: 10 minutes

Servings 8

Nutritional Values per serving: 187 Calories; 14.2g Fat; 5.2g Total Carbs; 9.4g Protein; 3.4g Sugars

Ingredients

- 1/2 pound rutabaga, grated
- 4 slices meaty bacon, chopped
- 7 ounces Gruyère cheese, shredded
- 3 eggs, beaten
- 3 tablespoons almond flour
- 1 teaspoon granulated garlic
- 1 teaspoon shallot powder
- Sea salt and ground black pepper, to taste

Directions

1. Add 1 cup of water and a metal trivet to the Instant Pot.
2. Mix all of the above ingredients until everything is well incorporated.
3. Put the mixture into a silicone pod tray that is previously greased with a nonstick cooking spray. Cover the tray with a sheet of aluminum foil and lower it onto the trivet.
4. Secure the lid. Choose "Manual" mode and Low pressure; cook for 5 minutes. Once cooking is complete, use a quick pressure release; carefully remove the lid. Bon appétit!

Juicy Meatballs

Preparation Time: 25 MIN

Serving: 8

Ingredients:

- 1 pound grass-fed ground chicken
- 1 organic egg
- 1/3 cup almond flour
- ½ tsp garlic powder
- Salt and freshly ground black pepper, to taste
- ¾ cup hot sauce
- 2 tbsp. olive oil
- 2 tbsp. melted butter
- ½ cup blue cheese dressing

Directions:

1. In a bowl, add all ingredients except, oil, hot sauce, butter and blue cheese dressing and mix until well combined.
2. Make equal sized meatballs from the mixture.
3. Place the oil in the Instant Pot and select "Sauté". Then add the meatballs and cook for about 4-5 minutes or until browned from all sides.

4. Meanwhile, in a bowl, mix together hot sauce and butter.
5. Select the "Cancel" and place butter mixture over meatballs.
6. Secure the lid and place the pressure valve to "Seal" position.
7. Select the "Poultry" and just use the default time of 5 minutes.
8. Select the "Cancel" and carefully do a Quick release.
9. Remove the lid and serve immediately with the topping of dressing.

Nutritional Values per serving:

Calories 278

Total Fat 21.6g

Net Carbs 0.33g

Protein 19g

Fiber 0.6g

Perfect Chicken Wings

Preparation Time: 40 MIN

Serving: 4

Ingredients:

- 1½ pounds grass-fed chicken wings
- ¼ cup sugar-free tomato puree
- 2-3 drops liquid stevia
- 1 tbsp. fresh lemon juice
- Salt and freshly ground black pepper, to taste

Directions:

1. In the bottom of Instant Pot, arrange a steamer trivet and pour 1 cup of water.
2. Place the pan on top of the trivet.
3. Place chicken wings on top of the trivet, standing vertically.
4. Secure the lid and place the pressure valve to "Seal" position.
5. Select "Manual" and cook under "High Pressure" for about 10 minutes.
6. Preheat the oven to broiler.
7. Select the "Cancel" and carefully do a Quick release.
8. Meanwhile, in a bowl, add remaining ingredients and beat until well combined.

9. Remove the lid and transfer chicken wings to the bowl of sauce.
10. Coat the wings with sauce generously.
11. Arrange the chicken wings onto a parchment paper lined baking sheet and broil for about 5 minutes.
12. Serve hot with remaining sauce.

Nutritional Values per serving:

Calories 330

Total Fat 12.7g

Net Carbs 0.37g

Protein 49.5g

Fiber 0.3g

2-Ingredients Chicken Wings

Preparation Time: 40 MIN

Serving: 6

Ingredients:

- 2 pounds grass-fed chicken wings and drumettes
- ½ cup sugar-free BBQ sauce

Directions:

1. In the bottom of Instant Pot, arrange a steamer basket and pour 1 cup of water.
2. Place the wings and drumettes into the steamer basket.
3. Secure the lid and place the pressure valve to "Seal" position.
4. Select "Manual" and cook under "High Pressure" for about 5 minutes.
5. Preheat the oven to 450 degrees F. Arrange a wire rack on a baking sheet.
6. Select the "Cancel" and carefully do a Natural release.
7. Remove the lid and transfer wings and drumettes to a large plate.
8. With paper towels, pat dry the wings and drumettes.
9. In a bowl, add wings and drumettes with BBQ sauce and toss to coat well.

10. Place the wings and drumettes onto the prepared baking sheet in a single layer.
11. Bake for about 8-15 minutes.
12. Remove from oven and serve warm.

Nutritional Values per serving:

Calories 319

Total Fat 11.3g

Net Carbs 1.26g

Protein 43.7g

Fiber 0.1g

Sticky Chicken Wings

Preparation Time: 40 MIN

Serving: 8

Ingredients:

- 3 pounds drum and wings separated grass-fed chicken wings
- 6 tbsp. olive oil (divided
- 1 cup sugar-free teriyaki sauce
- 1 tbsp. fresh lemon juice
- 1 tbsp. Erythritol
- ½ tsp crushed red pepper flakes

Directions:

1. In a large bowl, add chicken wings, 4 tablespoons of oil, teriyaki sauce, lemon juice and Erythritol and mix well.
2. Refrigerate for at least 2 hours.
3. Remove chicken wings from the bowl, reserving marinade.
4. Place the remaining oil in the Instant Pot and select "Sauté". Then add the wings and cook for about -4 minutes or until browned from all sides.
5. Select the "Cancel" and place reserved marinade over wings evenly.

6. Secure the lid and place the pressure valve to "Seal" position.
7. Select "Manual" and cook under "High Pressure" for about 7 minutes.
8. Preheat the oven to broiler.
9. Select the "Cancel" and carefully do a "Natural" release for about 10 minutes and then do a "Quick" release.
10. Remove the lid and transfer the wings onto a baking sheet in a single layer.
11. Broil for about 6-8 minutes.
12. Remove from oven and serve warm with the sprinkling of red pepper flakes.

Nutritional Values per serving:

Calories 446

Total Fat 23.2g

Net Carbs 0.95g

Protein 51.4g

Fiber 0.1g

Simple Boiled Peanuts

Preparation Time: 1½ HOUR

Serving: 6

Ingredients:

1 pound raw peanuts in the shell

1/3 cup coarse sea salt

Filtered water, as required

Directions:

1. Rinse the peanuts under cold running water and remove any twigs and roots.
2. In the bottom of Instant Pot, place peanuts, salt and enough water to cover the peanuts and stir.
3. Place a plate or trivet on top of peanuts.
4. Secure the lid and place the pressure valve to "Seal" position.
5. Select "Manual" and cook under "High Pressure" for about 80 minutes.
6. Select the "Cancel" and carefully do a "Natural" release.
7. Remove the lid and keep aside to cool.
8. Drain well and serve.

Nutritional Values per serving:

Calories 429

Total Fat 37.2g

Net Carbs 2.03g

Protein 19.5g

Fiber 6.4g

Southern Boiled Peanuts

Preparation Time: 1 HOUR 40 MIN

Serving: 6

Ingredients:

- 1 pound jumbo raw peanuts
- ½ cup sea salt
- 1 tbsp. Cajun seasoning
- Filtered water, as required

Directions:

1. Rinse the peanuts under cold running water and remove any twigs and roots.
2. In the bottom of Instant Pot, place peanuts, salt, Cajun seasoning and enough water to cover the peanuts and stir.
3. Place a plate or trivet on top of peanuts.
4. Secure the lid and place the pressure valve to "Seal" position.
5. Select "Manual" and cook under "High Pressure" for about 65-90 minutes.
6. Select the "Cancel" and carefully do a "Natural" release.
7. Remove the lid and keep aside to cool.
8. Drain well and serve.

Nutritional Values per serving:

Calories 429

Total Fat 37.2g

Net Carbs 2.03g

Protein 19.5g

Fiber 6.4g

Hard Boiled Eggs

Preparation Time: 10 MIN

Serving: 4

Ingredients:

- 8 large Eggs
- 1 cup Water

Instructions:

1. Set the wire rack in the Instant Pot and pour in the water.
2. Carefully place eggs in and place and lock the lid.
3. Manually set the cooking time to 4 minutes at high pressure.
4. Quick release the pressure and transfer the eggs in iced water for 5 minutes for easier peeling.
5. Use immediately or store in the fridge for later use.

Nutritional Values per serving:

Calories: 156

Total Fats: 10.6g

Net Carbs: 1.1g

Proteins: 12.6g

Fibers: 0g

Steamed Artichokes

Preparation Time: 20 MIN

Serving: 4

Ingredients:

- 4 medium Artichokes
- 1 wedge Lemon
- 1 cup Water

Directions:

1. Wash the artichokes well and with a knife cut off the stem and around an inch of the top.
2. Rub the cut on top with the lemon, to prevent browning, and gently spread the leaves a bit.
3. Place the artichokes in a steamer insert in the Instant Pot and pour in a cup of water.
4. Place and lock the lid, and set the Instant Pot manual to 10 minutes cooking time at high pressure.
5. When done let the Instant Pot naturally release the pressure for 10 minutes and then open the valve for quick release.
6. Serve warm with a dipping sauce.

Nutritional Values per serving:

Calories: 60

Total Fats: 0.2g

Net Carbs: 6.6g

Proteins: 4.2g

Fibers: 6.9g

Zingy Boiled Peanuts

Preparation Time: 1 HOUR 40 MIN

Serving: 6

Ingredients:

- 1 pound raw peanuts
- 1/3 cup Old Bay seasoning
- ¼ cup kosher salt
- ¼ cup apple cider vinegar
- 1 tbsp. mustard seeds
- 1 bay leaf
- Filtered water, as required

Directions:

1. Rinse the peanuts under cold running water and remove any twigs and roots.
2. In the bottom of Instant Pot, add all ingredients and enough water to cover the peanuts and stir.
3. Place a plate or trivet on top of peanuts.
4. Secure the lid and place the pressure valve to "Seal" position.
5. Select "Manual" and cook under "High Pressure" for about 75-90 minutes.
6. Select the "Cancel" and carefully do a "Natural" release.
7. Remove the lid and keep aside to cool.

8. Drain well and serve.

Nutritional Values per serving:

Calories 4540

Total Fat 37.8g

Net Carbs 0.48g

Protein 20g

Fiber 6.7g

Unique Party Food

Preparation Time: 18 MIN

Serving: 4

Ingredients:

- 1 pound asparagus spears
- 8-ounce sliced prosciutto

Directions:

1. Wrap the prosciutto slices around asparagus spears.
2. In the bottom of Instant Pot, arrange a steamer basket and pour 2 cups of water.
3. Place the carrots into the steamer basket.
4. Arrange any extra un-wrapped spears in the bottom of the steamer basket in a single layer.
5. Place prosciutto-wrapped asparagus on top in a single layer.
6. Secure the lid and place the pressure valve to "Seal" position.
7. Select "Manual" and cook under "High Pressure" for about 2-3 minutes.
8. Select the "Cancel" and carefully do a Natural release.
9. Remove the lid and serve warm

Nutritional Values per serving:

Calories 105

Total Fat 3.3g

Net Carbs 1.32 g

Protein 14.4g

Fiber 2,1g

Decadent Liver Pâté

Preparation Time: 25 MIN

Serving: 6

Ingredients:

- 1 tsp olive oil
- 1 roughly chopped medium yellow onion
- Salt and freshly ground black pepper, to taste
- ¾ pound grass-fed chicken livers
- 1 bay leaf
- ¼ cup homemade chicken broth
- 1 tbsp. fresh lemon juice
- 2 anchovies in oil
- 1 tbsp. capers
- 1 tbsp. butter

Directions:

1. Place the oil in the Instant Pot and select "Sauté". Then add the onion with a little salt and black pepper and cook for about 2-3 minutes.
2. Add the chicken livers and bay leaf and cook for about 2 minutes.
3. Add the broth and scrape brown bits from the bottom.
4. Select the "Cancel" and stir the mixture once.

5. Secure the lid and place the pressure valve to "Seal" position.
6. Select "Manual" and cook under "High Pressure" for about 5 minutes.
7. Select the "Cancel" and carefully do a Natural release.
8. Remove the lid and discard the bay leaf.
9. Stir in anchovies and capers and with a stick blender, blend the mixture until pureed.
10. Stir in butter and rum and transfer to a bowl.
11. Refrigerate to chill before serving.

Nutritional Values per serving:

Calories 142

Total Fat 7.3g

Net Carbs 0.4g

Protein 15.7g

Fiber 0.5g

Exotic Mushroom Pâté

Preparation Time: 25 MIN

Serving: 6

Ingredients:

- 1 cup boiling water
- ¾ cup rinsed dry porcini mushrooms
- 2 tbsp. unsalted butter
- 1 sliced small yellow onion
- 1 pound thinly sliced fresh cremini mushrooms
- 2-3 tbsp. homemade chicken broth
- 1 tbsp. fresh lemon juice
- 1 bay leaf
- Salt and ground white pepper, to taste
- 1 tbsp. extra-virgin olive oil
- 3 tbsp. finely grated Parmigiana Reggiano cheese

Directions:

1. In a heat-proof bowl, mix together boiling water and dry porcini mushrooms.
2. Cover the bowl tightly and keep aside.
3. Place the butter in the Instant Pot and select "Sauté". Then add the onion and cook for about 5 minutes.
4. Add the fresh mushrooms and cook for about 5 minutes.

5. Add broth and lemon juice and cook for about 5 minutes or until all the liquid is absorbed.
6. Select the "Cancel" and stir in porcini mushrooms and with soaking liquid, bay leaf, salt and black pepper.
7. Secure the lid and place the pressure valve to "Seal" position.
8. Select "Manual" and cook under "High Pressure" for about 12 minutes.
9. Select the "Cancel" and carefully do a Natural release.
10. Remove the lid and discard the bay leaf.
11. Add the olive oil and with an immersion blender, blend the mixture until smooth.
12. Add the cheese and blend until well combined.
13. Transfer the mixture to a bowl and refrigerate for about 2 hours before serving.

Nutritional Values per serving:

Calories 115

Total Fat 6.6g

Net Carbs 0.96g

Protein 6.3g

Fiber 0.7g

Garden Fresh Salsa

Preparation Time: 30 MIN

Serving: 20

Ingredients:

- 4 cups cored, peeled and chopped tomatoes
- 1 (15-ouncecan sugar-free tomato sauce
- 1 (6-ouncecan sugar-free tomato paste
- 1 chopped medium yellow onion
- 2 seeded and chopped large green bell peppers
- 3 seeded and chopped jalapeño peppers
- 4 minced garlic cloves
- ½ cup apple cider vinegar
- 1 tbsp. hot sauce
- 1 tbsp. ground cumin
- Kosher salt, to taste

Directions:

1. In the bottom of Instant Pot, place all ingredients and stir to combine.
2. Secure the lid and place the pressure valve to "Seal" position.
3. Select "Manual" and cook under "High Pressure" for about 15 minutes.
4. Select the "Cancel" and carefully do a "Natural" release.

5. Remove the lid and keep aside to cool for about 20 minutes.
6. Transfer the salsa into wide mouth pint jars and seal with lids.
7. Refrigerate to chill before serving.

Nutritional Values per serving:

Calories 29

Total Fat 0.3g

Net Carbs 0.30g

Protein 1.3g

Fiber 1.5g

Party Meatballs

Preparation Time: 40 MIN

Serving: 8

Ingredients:

- 1 pound lean ground turkey
- 1 organic egg
- ¼ tsp dried thyme
- ¼ tsp dried oregano
- ¼ tsp dried rosemary
- ¼ tsp garlic powder
- Salt and freshly ground black pepper, to taste
- 1½ cups sugar-free tomato sauce

Directions:

1. In a bowl, add all ingredients except tomato sauce and mix until well combined.
2. Make equal sized meatballs from the mixture.
3. In the bottom of Instant Pot, place meatballs and tomato sauce and gently stir to combine.
4. Secure the lid and place the pressure valve to "Seal" position.
5. Select "Manual" and cook under "High Pressure" for about 25 minutes.
6. Select the "Cancel" and carefully do a "Quick" release.

7. Remove the lid and serve.

Nutritional Values per serving:

Calories 101

Total Fat 4.7g

Net Carbs 0.18g

Protein 12.5g

Fiber 0.8g

Cheese Loaded Burgers

Preparation Time: 20 MIN

Serving: 2

Ingredients:

- 1 pound grass-fed lean ground beef
- 1 tbsp. Worcestershire sauce
- ¼ tsp garlic powder
- Salt and freshly ground black pepper, to taste
- 2-ounce shredded cheddar cheese

Directions:

1. In a large bowl, add ground beef, Worcestershire Sauce, garlic powder, salt and black pepper and mix until well combined.
2. Make 4 equal sized balls from the mixture.
3. With your hands, flatten each ball.
4. Place 1-ounce cheese in the center of 2 of the flattened balls.
5. Cover each with remaining 2 flatten balls, pressing the edges together well.
6. In the bottom of Instant Pot, arrange a steamer tray and pour ½ cup of water.
7. Place burgers on top of steamer tray.

8. Secure the lid and place the pressure valve to "Seal" position.
9. Select "Manual" and cook under "High Pressure" for about 5 minutes.
10. Select the "Cancel" and carefully do a "Natural" release.
11. Remove the lid and serve.

Nutritional Values per serving:

Calories 544

Total Fat 23.5g

Net Carbs 1g

Protein 75.9g

Fiber 0g

Mini Sausage Bites

Preparation Time: 20 MIN

Serving: 10

Ingredients:

- 2 pounds gluten-free cut into 1/3-inch thick slices Kielbasa links
- 1 cup sugar-free BBQ sauce
- ½ cup filtered water

Directions:

1. In the bottom of Instant Pot, place all ingredients and stir to combine.
2. Secure the lid and place the pressure valve to "Seal" position.
3. Select "Manual" and cook under "High Pressure" for about 5 minutes.
4. Select the "Cancel" and carefully do a "Natural" release for about 10 minutes and then do a "Quick" release.
5. Remove the lid and transfer the mixture to a serving bowl.
6. Keep aside for about 10-15 minutes before serving.

Nutritional Values per serving:

Calories 243

Total Fat 16g

Net Carbs 1.26g

Protein 11.9g

Fiber 0.2g

Refreshing Curd

Preparation time: 10 minutes

Cooking time: 5 minutes

Servings: 4

Ingredients:

- 3 tablespoons stevia
- 12 ounces raspberries
- 2 egg yolks
- 2 tablespoons lemon juice
- 2 tablespoons ghee

Directions:

1. Put raspberries in your instant pot, add stevia and lemon juice, stir, cover and cook on High for 2 minutes.
2. Strain this into a bowl, add egg yolks, stir well and return to your pot.
3. Set the pot on Simmer mode, cook for 2 minutes, add ghee, stir well, transfer to a container and serve cold.
4. Enjoy!

Nutritional Values per serving: Calories 132, fat 1, fiber 0, carbs 2, protein 4

The Best Jam Ever

Preparation time: 10 minutes

Cooking time: 5 minutes

Servings: 6

Ingredients:

- 4 and ½ cups peaches, peeled and cubed
- 4 tablespoons stevia
- ¼ cup crystallized ginger, chopped

Directions:

1. Set your instant pot on Simmer mode, add peaches, ginger and stevia, stir, bring to a boil, cover and cook on High for 5 minutes.
2. Divide into bowls and serve cold.
3. Enjoy!

Nutritional Values per serving: Calories 53, fat 0, fiber 0, carbs 0, protein 2

Divine Pears

Preparation time: 10 minutes

Cooking time: 4 minutes

Servings: 12

Ingredients:

- 8 pears, cored and cut into quarters
- 1 teaspoon cinnamon powder
- 2 apples, peeled, cored and cut into quarters
- ¼ cup natural apple juice

Directions:

1. In your instant pot, mix pears with apples, cinnamon and apple juice, stir, cover and cook on High for 4 minutes.
2. Blend using an immersion blender, divide into small jars and serve cold
3. Enjoy!

Nutritional Values per serving: Calories 100, fat 0, fiber 0, carbs 0, protein 2

Berry Marmalade

Preparation time: 10 minutes

Cooking time: 20 minutes

Servings: 12

Ingredients:

- 1 pound cranberries
- 1 pound strawberries
- ½ pound blueberries
- ounces black currant
- 4 tablespoons stevia
- Zest from 1 lemon
- A pinch of salt
- 2 tablespoon water

Directions:

1. In your instant pot, mix strawberries with cranberries, blueberries, currants, lemon zest, stevia and water, stir, cover and cook on High for 10 minutes.
2. Divide into jars and serve cold.
3. Enjoy!

Nutritional Values per serving: Calories 87, fat 2, fiber 0, carbs 1, protein 2

Orange Delight

Preparation time: 10 minutes

Cooking time: 25 minutes

Servings: 8

Ingredients:

- Juice from 2 lemons
- 6 tablespoons stevia
- 1 pound oranges, peeled and halved
- 1-pint water

Directions:

1. In your instant pot, mix lemon juice with orange juice and orange segments, water and stevia, cover and cook on High for 15 minutes.
2. Divide into jars and serve cold.

Nutritional Values per serving: Calories 75, fat 0, fiber 0, carbs 2, protein 2

Simple Squash Pie

Preparation time: 10 minutes

Cooking time: 14 minutes

Serving: 8

Ingredients:

- 2 pounds butternut squash, peeled and chopped
- 2 eggs
- 2 cups water
- 1 cup coconut milk
- 2 tablespoons honey
- 1 teaspoon cinnamon powder
- ½ teaspoon ginger powder
- ¼ teaspoon cloves, ground
- 1 tablespoon arrowroot powder
- Chopped pecans

Directions:

1. Put 1 cup water in your instant pot, add the steamer basket, add squash pieces, cover, cook on High for 4 minutes, drain, transfer to a bowl and mash.
2. Add honey, milk, eggs, cinnamon, ginger and cloves, stir very well and pour into ramekins.
3. Add the rest of the water to your instant pot, add the steamer basket, add ramekins inside, cover and cook on High for 10 minutes.
4. Garnish with chopped pecans and serve.
5. Enjoy!

Nutritional Values per serving: Calories 132, fat 1, fiber 2, carbs 2, protein 3

Winter Pudding

Preparation time: 10 minutes

Cooking time: 40 minutes

Servings: 4

Ingredients:

- 4 ounces dried cranberries, soaked for a few hours and drained
- 2 cups water
- 4 ounces apricots, chopped
- 1 cup coconut flour
- 3 teaspoons baking powder
- 3 tablespoons stevia
- 1 teaspoon ginger powder
- A pinch of cinnamon powder
- 15 tablespoons ghee
- 3 tablespoons maple syrup
- 4 eggs
- 1 carrot, grated

Directions:

1. In a blender, mix flour with baking powder, stevia, cinnamon and ginger and pulse a few times.
2. Add ghee, maple syrup, eggs, carrots, cranberries and apricots, stir and spread into a greased pudding pan.
3. Add the water to your instant pot, add the steamer basket, add the pudding, cover and cook on High for 30 minutes.
4. Leave pudding to cool down before serving.
5. Enjoy!

Nutritional Values per serving: Calories 213, fat 2, fiber 1, carbs 3, protein 3

Banana Dessert

Preparation time: 10 minutes

Cooking time: 30 minutes

Servings: 6

Ingredients:

- 2 tablespoons stevia
- 1/3 cup ghee, soft
- 1 teaspoon vanilla
- 1 egg
- 2 bananas, mashed
- 1 teaspoon baking powder
- 1 and ½ cups coconut flour
- ½ teaspoons baking soda
- 1/3 cup coconut milk
- 2 cups water
- Cooking spray

Directions:

1. In a bowl, mix milk stevia, ghee, egg, vanilla and bananas and stir everything.
2. In another bowl, mix flour with salt, baking powder and soda.
3. Combine the 2 mixtures, stir well and pour into a greased cake pan.
4. Add the water to your pot, add the steamer basket, add the cake pan, cover and cook at High for 30 minutes.
5. Leave cake to cool down, slice and serve.
6. Enjoy!

Nutritional Values per serving: Calories 243, fat 1, fiber 1, carbs 2, protein 4

Apple Cake

Preparation time: 10 minutes

Cooking time: 1 hour and 10 minutes

Servings: 6

Ingredients:

- 3 cups apples, cored and cubed
- 1 cup water
- 3 tablespoons stevia
- 1 tablespoon vanilla
- 2 eggs
- 1 tablespoon apple pie spice
- 2 cups coconut flour
- 1 tablespoon baking powder
- 1 tablespoon ghee

Directions:
1. In a bowl mix eggs with ghee, apple pie spice, vanilla, apples and stevia and stir using your mixer.
2. In another bowl, mix baking powder with flour, stir, add to apple mix, stir again well and transfer to a cake pan.
3. Add 1 cup water to your instant pot, add the steamer basket, add cake pan, cover and cook at High for 1 hour and 10 minutes.
4. Cool cake down, slice and serve it.
5. Enjoy!

Nutritional Values per serving: Calories 100, fat 2, fiber 1, carbs 2, protein 2

Special Vanilla Dessert

Preparation time: 10 minutes

Cooking time: 10 minutes

Servings: 4

Ingredients:

- 1 cup almond milk
- 4 tablespoons flax meal
- 2 tablespoons coconut flour
- 2 and ½ cups water
- 2 tablespoons stevia
- 1 teaspoon espresso powder
- 2 teaspoons vanilla extract
- Coconut cream for serving

Directions:

1. In your instant pot, mix flax meal with flour, water, stevia, milk and espresso powder, stir, cover and cook on high for 10 minutes.
2. Add vanilla extract, stir well, leave aside for 5 minutes, divide into bowls and serve with coconut cream on top.
3. Enjoy!

Nutritional Values per serving: Calories 182, fat 2, fiber 1, carbs 3, protein 4

Tasty and Amazing Pear Dessert

Preparation time: 10 minutes

Cooking time: 6 minutes

Servings: 4

Ingredients:

- 1 cup water
- 2 cups pear, peeled and cubed
- 2 cups coconut milk
- 1 tablespoon ghee
- ¼ cups brown stevia
- ½ teaspoon cinnamon powder
- 4 tablespoons flax meal
- ½ cup walnuts, chopped
- ½ cup raisins

Directions:

1. In a heat proof dish, mix milk with stevia, ghee, flax meal, cinnamon, raisins, pears and walnuts and stir.
2. Put the water in your instant pot, add the steamer basket, place heat proof dish inside, cover and cook on High for 6 minutes.
3. Divide this great dessert into small cups and serve cold.
4. Enjoy!

Nutritional Values per serving: Calories 162, fat 3, fiber 1, carbs 2, protein 6

Cranberries Jam

Preparation time: 10 minutes

Cooking time: 15 minutes

Servings: 12

Ingredients:

- 16 ounces cranberries
- 4 ounces raisins
- 3 ounces water+ ¼ cup water
- 8 ounces figs
- 16 ounces strawberries, chopped
- Zest from 1 lemon

Directions:

1. Put figs in your blender, add ¼ cup water, pulse well and strain into a bowl.
2. In your instant pot, mix strawberries with cranberries, lemon zest, raisins, 3 ounces water and figs puree, stir, cover the pot, cook at High for 15 minutes, divide into small jars and serve.

Nutritional Values per serving: Calories 73, fat 1, fiber 1, carbs 2, protein 3

Lemon Jam

Preparation time: 10 minutes

Cooking time: 12 minutes

Servings: 8

Ingredients:

- 2 pounds lemons, sliced
- 2 cups dates
- 1 cup water
- 1 tablespoon vinegar

Directions:

1. Put dates in your blender, add water and pulse really well.
2. Put lemon slices in your instant pot, add dates paste and vinegar, stir, cover and cook on High for 12 minutes.
3. Stir, divide into small jars and serve.
4. Enjoy!

Nutritional Values per serving: Calories 72, fat 2, fiber 1, carbs 2, protein 6

Special Dessert

Preparation time: 10 minutes

Cooking time: 25 minutes

Servings: 4

Ingredients:

- 3 cups rooibos tea
- 1 tablespoon cinnamon, ground
- 2 cups cauliflower, riced
- 2 apples, diced
- 1 teaspoon cloves, ground
- 1 teaspoon turmeric, ground
- A drizzle of honey

Directions:

1. Put cauliflower rice in your instant pot, add tea, stir, cover and cook at High for 10 minutes
2. Add cinnamon, apples, turmeric and cloves, stir, cover and cook at High for 10 minutes mode.
3. Divide into bowls, drizzle honey on top and serve.
4. Enjoy!

www.ingramcontent.com/pod-product-compliance
Lightning Source LLC
Chambersburg PA
CBHW071821080526
44589CB00012B/873